OLD CAR WRECKS

and the vehicles at accident scenes, 1920s to 1960s

Ron Kowalke

Published by

krause publications

700 E. State Street • Iola, WI 54990-0001
Telephone: 715/445-2214

Please call or write for our free catalog.
Our toll-free number to place an order or obtain a free catalog is 800-258-0929
or please use our regular business telephone 715-445-2214
for editorial comment and further information.

Library of Congress Catalog Number: 90-60581

ISBN: 0-87341-510-8

Printed in the United States of America

Contents

On the covers:

Front: 1953 Pontiac (Peter Kanze photo), 1929 Ford Model AA service car (Old Cars photo), early ambulance from Bolmer Motor Car Co. of New Jersey (Old Cars photo)

Back: 1950s Brockway tractor with trailer (Peter Kanze photo), Late-1950s/early-1960s Triumph TR-3A (Ronald Marzlock photo)

Acknowledgments

This book was created from historic accident photographs contributed by many generous individuals. Several of these photos were peeled directly from the pages of family scrapbooks. A portion of the photos used are from the collections of Stephen Behling, Larry Burwell, Bruce Craig Historical Race Photos, Lawrence Gaddis/Martin Best, Phil Hall, Peter Kanze, Ronald Marzlock and William K. Miller. Special thanks go out to a group of readers of *Old Cars Weekly News & Marketplace* who, collectively, supplied the majority of the photos used as well as the interesting stories behind the wrecked vehicles depicted in the photos. Also, a thank you goes to Mark Patrick of the National Automotive History Collection at the Detroit Public Library. His suggestions on reference books proved invaluable to completing this book. Also, *Old Cars* staffers Ken Buttolph, Chad Elmore and Jim Lenzke deserve a big thank you for helping to identify many of the mangled vehicles in the photos. And last, but definitely not least, a special thanks to *Old Cars* Editorial Director John Gunnell. He authored the original *Antique Auto Wrecks* book in 1990, which provided the inspiration for this sequel.

A coupe lover's dream shop, several of the five-window wonders were undergoing repairs in this 1930s body shop. Note the sign in the background, which reads: Visitors and Collectors (bill collectors, we presume) Positively Not Allowed To Call On Employees During Work Hours. (Phil Evans photo)

Foreword

A book detailing auto accidents, or more appropriately the aftermath of auto accidents, may seem a bit macabre at first glance. But, the fact is, accidents have been a part of motoring history since the introduction of the motor-car. The field of motor vehicle accident investigation also has a long and distinguished history. And, when looked at within the context of improving our society, accident investigation is as important — and interesting — as the study of planets and the universe in the field of astronomy or the study of marine life and the seas in the field of oceanography. In other words, the photographs presented in this book represent, in part, a history lesson on the world of motoring during the 1920s to 1960s. Included in this window-view study of early motoring mishaps is a focus on vehicle construction — i.e.: the strengths and weaknesses of automobiles of that time period. Also covered is how outside forces such as road conditions and weather played a part in many accidents as well as how human behavior (or maybe, more appropriately, misbehavior) was also a catalyst for crashes.

The pictures presented in this book in no way depict human tragedy. No bodies, no blood, no gore. While that type of photograph exists in great number — and it is agreed that to motivate people to drive more responsibly, the gorier the photo the more effective it would be — this book and this foreword were not written to "preach" safe driving habits. Although, if in some way reading this book causes even one reader to remember to buckle up (or have seat belts installed in an older collector vehicle) or have his or her automobile safety inspected, that's great.

No, the subtle, underlying theme of this book is that driving a motor vehicle was, is and always will be a dangerous proposition. No amount of preaching about driving safely nor driver's education, for that matter, is going to help someone who intends to drive a car while registering a blood alcohol content of .20. Yet, it happens every day. Nor would safety tips and manuals do a bit of good for someone who ignores hazardous road conditions such as rain (hydroplaning) or snow and continues to travel at or above posted speed limits. Yet, it happens every day. Nor does advice or education do much good for those who conduct all kinds of business while driving their cars such as eating, talking on a cellular phone, applying makeup, reading a newspaper, etc., and fail to take care of the business at hand, which is attentively driving their automobile or truck. Yet, these are all common activities on our nation's roads.

The hoped-for message that readers will absorb from this book and retain for all time is this: Driving, whether it is done in a car old or new, truck big or small, motorcycle American-made or foreign, is a privilege. And if done responsibly, it can be a pleasurable activity for driver and passenger(s) as well as for those around us on the road. But because there were, are and always will be "offensive" — i.e.: inattentive, rude or risk-taker — drivers who have, in our democracy, obtained a driver's license, the need for defensive driving skills has always been, is and will always be essential. And if this book becomes the impetus for a defensive driving groundswell — or even better, a trendy new defensive driving public relations campaign with a catchy slogan such as "Defensive Driving, Do It For Life" — that'd be great, too.

But let's not get ahead of ourselves (a defensive driving tactic in itself). Being a defensive driver incorporates the practices of safe driving, such as buckling up and making sure our vehicles are road ready (i.e.: properly inflated tires with good tread, working brakes, headlights and horn, etc.). But it also encompasses being skilled enough to regain control of a vehicle that has just been pitched into the oncoming lane of traffic after hitting a pothole or skidding on a patch of ice. It's knowing how to react decisively when the drunk driver allows his car to veer into your lane at 60 mph or a doe and her two fawns decide to skitter across the highway just in front of your car.

There are numerous schools in Canada and the United States — as well as overseas — that use road racing courses or large expanses of asphalt to teach wet and dry defensive driving tactics to law enforcement personnel and chauffeurs. Many of these schools are also open to the public, and the cost of attending is reasonable when considering what is taught. Why not get the members of your car club to attend one as a weekend group activity? Maybe, if you'd ask, the instructors would allow members to bring their collector cars for some instruction on defensive driving in an older vehicle.

Studying the photographs in this book, it becomes clear that some accidents were unavoidable no matter how skilled and agile the drivers involved may have been. But defensive driving skills and a mindset of always expecting the unexpected would have, without a doubt, prevented some of the crashes depicted in this book. With modern roadways becoming more congested due to increasing amounts of traffic each year, the defensive driving posture will not be faddish nor will the expense of defensive driving schooling be a short-term investment.

And just in case you're the statistic lover and need reinforcement through numbers, by the time you finish reading this sentence there will have been five motor vehicle accidents in the United States. Think about it!

On the back of this photo was written: "Ruins of auto that crashed into telegraph pole in Watertown, Mass., March 1st, 1917, at 1:30 a.m. One man killed." (John Greenland photo)

There was bozo from Whipsocket,

Who thought that his car was a rocket.

He cut in and shot out,

Puttin' traffic to rout,

Till a crash and spill made him stop it.

Stay Alive - 1928

Marcus Dow speaking as Jim the Truckman

The Good Samaritan

James E. Malone of Macon, Ga., writes: "The accident pictured below happened in November 1954. The car with its top sheared off was a beautiful maroon (high luster) 1950 Dodge Coronet with U.S. Royal Master whitewall tires (curb resistant).

"I was a senior varsity football player for Perry High School and our school colors were maroon and gold. For each game, the car was made immaculate and decorated with gold trim. My parents drove it to the games in a motorcade and I got to drive it after the game.

"That November night, with my older sister recovering from a tonsil operation, my family went to visit my older brother in Warner Robins, Georgia, 15 miles away. They expected to return later than my football curfew so I stayed home.

"Returning from visiting my brother, my father drove cautiously through 'pea soup' fog over the same road he took daily to work. Approaching an expected, rural T-intersection, he searched for the luminous stop sign. The sign had been knocked down in a previous accident that night, and my father went through the intersection and over an embankment on the other side of the road. (This intersection is now a four-way and the hub of Centerville, Georgia).

"The Dodge's rear wheels would not get traction, which meant it would have to be towed out. The November night air was cold and damp, and a threat to my sister's recuperation. A good samaritan from Macon, Georgia, who came upon the Dodge offered to take my father, mother, sister and three younger brothers home. Totally out of context for my father, he accepted the ride from a stranger going 45 miles out of his way.

"This stranger saved six lives with his act of kindness as just minutes after pulling away from the stuck Dodge, a drunk driving the new 1954 Ford (pictured behind the Dodge) also went over the embankment traveling in excess of 100 miles per hour! The car climbed the rear of the Dodge and drove over it, shearing off its top, which acted like a bulldozer blade on the front of the Ford cutting a path through dense brush and going through trees too narrow for the Ford to pass. The Ford was damaged up front but its sides were not even scratched!

"Arriving home, my father (not yet aware of the accident) called our dealer to retrieve the Dodge. The dealer, Cecil Moody, was a friend and personally drove the tow truck to the embankment. I broke football curfew to drive with Mr. Moody and my father to retrieve the Dodge.

"Between the time the drunk crashed into the Dodge and our arriving at the accident scene, two more cars went through the intersection and over the embankment — lights flashed and confusion reigned. The Dodge was not were it got stuck.

"Through the dense fog, flashlight in hand, Mr. Moody called out, 'Your car is over here.' My father answered, 'No Cecil, I didn't have a convertible.'

"Later, the Ford was repaired requiring a new frame and front end. The Dodge was totaled, but thanks to the kindness of that stranger six family members were saved from certain death and the drunk driver was saved from being charged with six counts of vehicular manslaughter.

"The Dodge was the first car I drove by myself and losing it was like losing a friend."

The 1950 Dodge Coronet after the accident where the Ford (behind) drove over the Dodge tearing its top off. The Ford was repaired and put back on the road. (James E. Malone photo)

If the six members of the Malone family had been in the Dodge at the time the Ford drove over it, it would have been disastrous. The kind deed of a stranger kept them from harm. (James E. Malone photo)

Rugged Ford free-fall

Timothy C. Hall of Littleton, Colo., writes: "This accident occurred on June 8, 1950. My grandfather was driving what we called the 'old gray car', a 1940 Ford home from a Sunday dinner with relatives. My grandmother and I were in the back seat. I was 3-1/2 years old at the time. Gramps fell asleep at the wheel as we approached a bridge while entering the hamlet of Glenwood in Lenox Township, Susquehanna County, Pennsylvania.

"The car went up over a stone wall that was erected as a guard rail, adjacent to the bridge, flipped upside down in midair, and free-fell 15-20 feet to the ground landing on its top. The rear wheels were ripped off as we went over the stone wall. Customers from the nearby general store across the river heard the crash and came running and extracted us in a matter of moments.

"While the car was totaled, we all survived. My grandparents suffered serious injuries from which they recovered. I was unscathed, except for the finger marks on my chest from my grandmother's hand as she held me tightly through the whole ordeal. Of course there were no seat belts or airbags to buffer the impact of our crash. We owe our survival to the rugged construction of the cars of that era, and to luck. My grandfather wasn't so lucky though — he received a ticket from the state police for reckless driving."

Ground level view of the Ford showing how well the roof held up after the car fell almost 20 feet. (Timothy C. Hall photo)

Rear view showing Ford resting against bridge's stone foundation. (Timothy C. Hall photo)

Overhead view showing the huge rocks the Ford narrowly missed upon landing upside down. Note missing rear wheels, which were torn off in the ride over the bridge wall. (Timothy C. Hall photo)

"Wrecklamation"

Leon Bowers of Kirksville, Mo., presented us with a unique before and after photo opportunity that allows for a bit of balance to the carnage presented throughout this book. A rebuilder of wrecked cars since age 14 — he's now 65 years young — Leon sent pictures of two wrecked cars, as we requested, but also supplied photos of how the cars appeared after he (body)worked his magic on them. From the after photos it's evident Leon does quality work and his reclamation of automobiles from an early demise is appreciated.

Leon Bowers writes: "I was the driver of this 1940 Chevrolet Special Deluxe. In 1948, at an intersection, a two-ton truck ran a stop sign and we collided. I was lucky; I didn't get a scratch. There were no seat belts or airbags in 1948." (Leon Bowers photo)

Leon Bowers writes: "This 1959 Chevrolet was wrecked seven days before show day on the way to storing it. It had only seven miles on its odometer." The two youngsters in the "after" photo were not identified but the young man is holding a pair of sponge dice usually seen hanging from a car's rear view mirror. (Leon Bowers photo)

Building a smarter dummy

Within the auto industry through the years, Detroit has spawned numerous celebrities such as John DeLorean, Lee Iacocca and marque "founding fathers" such as Henry Ford, Louis Chevrolet and Walter Chrysler. But these giants never achieved the level of fame garnered by a pair of "working stiffs" whose faces have been splashed across billboards nationwide, whose likenesses have been made into children's toy dolls and who have starred in numerous television and radio commercials promoting the use of seat belts and safe driving in general. And the fact that they're a couple of dummies hasn't hurt their celebrity status. These two well-known and oft-abused stars are Vince and Larry, the crash test dummy spokesmannequins.

Most of us would categorize Vince and Larry as cute and comical. But what they represent as auto industry tools used to measure the forces that occur inside a purposely crashed vehicle and how those forces affect the human body would more properly fall into the categories of ugly and brutal. By having dummies "sit-in" in place of humans or animals when crash testing of automobiles is conducted, valuable information can be safely gleaned from this testing to help Detroit — and the world — build safer automobiles.

At first, it might seem pointless to use mannequins such as Vince and Larry in crash testing. How much information can be learned from something that doesn't speak and can't relate what happened during the impacts of crash testing? Well, in a manner of speaking, crash test dummies let their bodies do their talking. A modern crash test dummy doesn't deserve that crude moniker because it is a sophisticated robot-like creature that simulates the human body and how flesh and bone are taxed during auto accidents.

How sophisticated a crash test dummy really is becomes apparent when it is identified by its real name — Anthropomorphic Test Device, or ATD for short.

It wasn't always this way. The origin of the crash test dummy is credited to the U.S. Air Force, which used canvas sacks filled with sand as "stand-in" pilots in flight simulation exercises in the late 1940s. Later, Detroit's use of crash test "dummies" included cadavers, baboons and pigs having the trauma of accident testing inflicted upon them to measure the results. But, due to public outcry from groups such as animal rights activists Detroit discontinued this controversial practice.

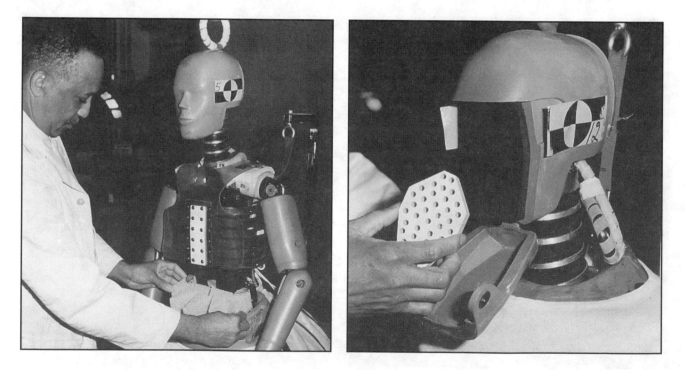

Foam inserts in General Motors' crash dummy heads and abdomens are helping the automaker better understand injury forces in real-world accidents. Safety engineers use these "frangible" inserts, made of construction grade foam, to show the force of a crash on these parts of the anatomy. There is a tell-tale deflection on the inserts that correlates closely with injury in car crashes. Medical researchers at GM have been able to calculate just how much force it takes to deform the body and cause injury. Use of the foam inserts in dummy tests allows safety engineers to more precisely design safety belts and airbags to protect real drivers and passengers. (General Motors photos)

In the early 1970s, General Motors was credited with inventing the electronic mannequin for use as a crash test dummy. This unit was named the Hybrid II. Vince and Larry are both an improved Hybrid III version of the crash test dummy, which has been used since 1987. A Hybrid III model can measure 85 different variables in a crash, and give detailed information on the impact's effect on the head and chest, neck, spine, knee and thigh.

The Hybrid III model costs in excess of $100,000 each. And, as with everything else in Detroit, a new model is just around the corner. The next evolution of the ATD is the TAD, or Trauma Assessment Device. These "advanced dummies" will allow for more refined data to be acquired from crash tests, not to mention that with TAD the opportunity will exist for a new celebrity spokesmannequin to allow Vince and Larry to retire and heal some old wounds!

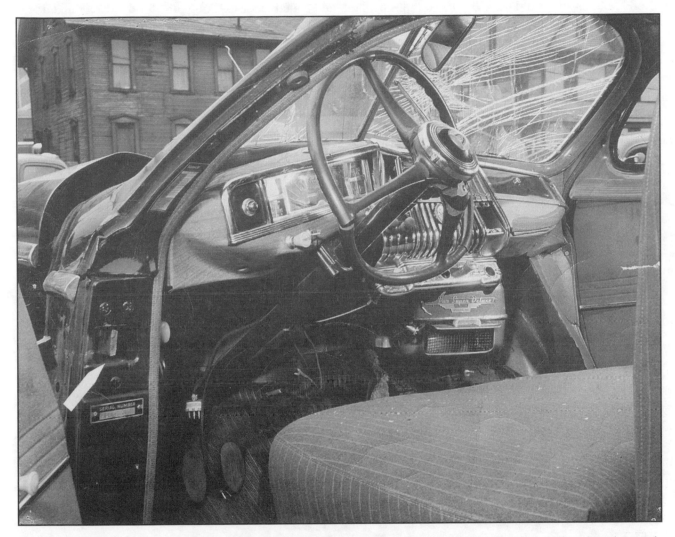

Several injury-causing items are evident in this interior shot of a 1930s car that was involved in a head-on collision. With no seat belts to restrain occupants during the crash, they were hurtled forward on impact. Aside from the obvious impact against the steering wheel, the dash is full of knobs and sharp edges that could do serious harm to the human body. Head injuries due to impact with the windshield were also commonplace during this period. Also, note the broken door hinge (arrow). Doors flying open during an accident, due to car body/chassis flexing and the primitive design of latching mechanisms, also spelled doom for many who were ejected from a crashing vehicle. This was especially true in roll-over accidents. (Lloyd A. Himes photo)

Siren song

Vehicle accident scenes are filled with chaos. Amid the smoking, twisted wreckage the priority is to extricate the injured and rush them via ambulance to the hospital. As depicted in two of the photographs in this section, that rush by the ambulance crew to perform its duty and help save lives can be chaotic in itself, with the ambulance being involved in a crash en route to or leaving an accident scene.

In the United States, non-horsedrawn ambulances have been dispatched to accident scenes since approximately the turn of the century. According to Katherine Traver Barkley, in her book titled *The Ambulance*, the first motor ambulance, an electrically-powered vehicle, was used by a Chicago hospital in 1899. It weighed 1,600 pounds and could travel up to 16 miles per hour and contained a speaking tube for the driver and doctor onboard to communicate.

According to *American Funeral Cars & Ambulances* by Thomas A. McPherson, the majority of the pre-1920 motor ambulances in this country were "assembled" coaches. This meant that all the components such as the running gear and associated pieces had to be gathered from one or more sources and then installed in a maker's chassis and specially-built body. By the early 1920s, coachbuilders were using the manufactured chassis of the larger passenger automobiles or light-duty trucks from makers such as Buick, Packard, Pierce-Arrow and Studebaker.

Through the early 1970s, McPherson's book lists 162 companies in both the United States and Canada that have been involved in vehicle conversions to ambulances/funeral cars. This list includes the more famous conversion houses such as Sayers & Scovill, which later evolved into Hess & Eisenhardt, S & S; Miller-Meteor; and Superior Coach Corp., all three of Ohio and Flxible Co. of Canada. Also listed is Harley-Davidson Co., which built motorcycle ambulances and the Auburn Automobile Co. of Indiana, which built ambulances in the mid-1930s.

As of the late-1970s, according to Barkley, the breakdown of ambulance types was, in descending order: conventional (purpose-built) units (36 percent), station wagons (24 percent), hearses (dual-purpose vehicles - 21 percent); panel trucks (10 percent); and rescue vehicles (9 percent). Also, what equipment an ambulance carried consisted of: oxygen unit (62 percent), backboards (30 percent), splints (65 percent), sterile gauze (81 percent), bag-mask resuscitator (46 percent), universal dressing (54 percent) and adhesive tape (77 percent).

By comparison, the modern "superambulance," staffed by paramedics or emergency medical technicians, allows for care that equals an emergency room on wheels. Past or present, though, whatever the siren song, it will always be a comforting sound to an injury victim at the accident scene.

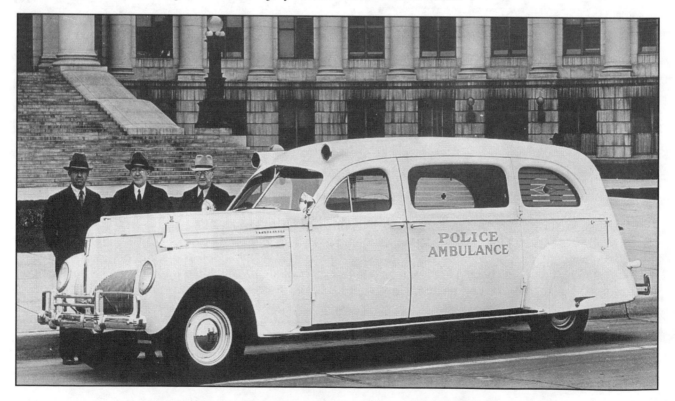

The Bender Body Corp. of Cleveland, Ohio, transformed 1938-1940 Studebakers (this is a 1939 model) into ambulances. This particular model was called the Samaritan. What police department this particular ambulance was attached to is unknown, as are the identities of the three gentlemen posing with the vehicle. (Studebaker photo)

A right-hand drive ambulance from the teens is posed in front of the Bolmer Motor Car Co. of Bound Brook, N.J. Bolmer dealt in Chalmers and Hupmobiles, and with the Bolmer logo so prominent on the side of the ambulance it was probably outfitted and donated by the dealership for use in that New Jersey city. (Old Cars photo)

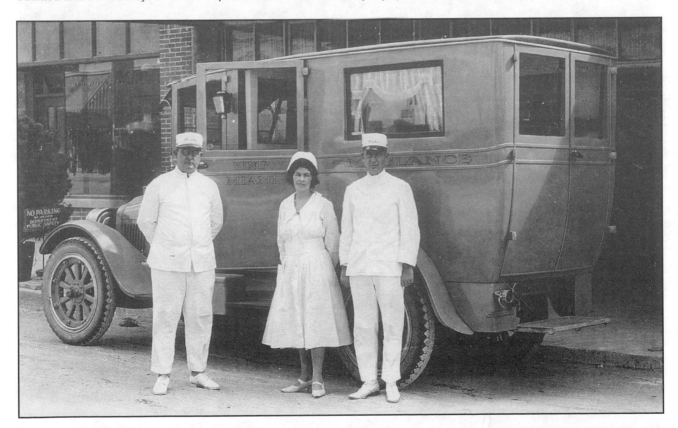

A formal-looking ambulance crew of the King Undertaking Co. pose with what appears to be an early-1920s Packard modified for ambulance duty. Based in Miami, Fla., those high-collared, long-sleeved uniforms must have made for some uncomfortable duty in summertime. (Old Cars photo)

The U.S. Army medical department at Selfridge Field, Mich., used this 1929 Buick modified for ambulance duty by Flxible of Ohio to transport injured soldiers. (Old Cars photo)

This 1930 Buick/Flxible ambulance was operated by the U.S. Public Health Service and based at the Marine Hospital. Note the ornate leaded glasswork that identifies this vehicle as an ambulance in the rear quarter window. (Old Cars photo)

One distinguishing feature of this 1931 Buick/Flxible ambulance is the alarm siren mounted out front above the bumper to alert traffic to move out of the way. The rear quarter window also carries an ornate design symbolizing this as an emergency vehicle. (Old Cars photo)

Displayed at an auto show, this 1948 Chevrolet was modified for ambulance duty by Barnette coachworks of Memphis, Tenn. (Applegate and Applegate photo)

The drive to or from the accident scene can be hazardous to an ambulance crew as evidenced by this wrecked 1937 Cadillac ambulance operated by the Chillum-Adelphi Volunteer Fire Department in Prince Georges County, Md. The faded graphics on the door probably mean this emergency vehicle saw duty elsewhere and was purchased used by the Maryland volunteer fire unit. (Lawrence J. Gaddis/Martin L. Best photo)

Ambulance #23 of the Kansas City Health Department was involved in a head-on crash on Jan. 19, 1946. The 1940 Ford was demolished, but amazingly its hood-mounted warning light survived intact. (William K. Miller photo)

The Kansas City (Missouri) Health Department maintained a fleet of ambulances in the mid-1930s, all of which were Fords, as well as a Ford Model BB tow truck. Note the warning sirens and warning lights mounted out front on each ambulance. (William K. Miller photo)

A uniformed staff of 15 ambulance crew employed by the Kansas City Health Department pose with #25 and #36 of the fleet of Ford ambulances maintained by the department circa 1940. Speculating, the gentleman in the middle could be a physician or a dispatcher and he's hiding a tobacco product (pipe?) in his pocket as it would not be good for a member of the health department to be photographed smoking. (William K. Miller photo)

Based on the Series 22 chassis and priced at $6,119, this Packard was transformed for ambulance duty by the Henney Co. of Freeport, Ill. Note the military-like uniforms worn by the ambulance crew. (Applegate and Applegate photo)

This 1950 Cadillac modified for ambulance duty by A.J. Miller Co. of Ohio featured frosted glass in the rear quarter windows as standard. Price for this vehicle sans options was $6,190. Optional equipment shown is the Federal combination roof warning light siren and roof-mounted warning light pods. (Applegate and Applegate photo)

A possible Barnette conversion was this 1951 Chevrolet, being offered for sale at an auction in Tulsa, Okla., in 1987. (Old Cars photo)

A 1955 Studebaker Conestoga was transformed into this ambulet attached to a community's fire department. Note the raised window portion of the split tailgate to facilitate the loading of injury victims. (Old Cars photo)

This 1956 Cadillac is badged as a Miller conversion, but the A.J. Miller Co. was purchased by the Wayne Works, makers of Meteor ambulances and funeral coaches, in 1956 and later renamed Miller-Meteor Co. The Cadillac featured tunnel-type roof lights above the windshield and roof marker lights at the rear. (Applegate and Applegate)

Conversion of this 1958 Buick to ambulance duty was performed by National of Indiana. The vehicle, which features tunnel-type roof lights front and rear, is owned by Gene Reynolds of New York. (Old Cars photo)

Studebaker's Lark VIII for 1959 was also offered in ambulet configuration. At this angle a good view is offered of the gurney loaded into tight quarters. (Studebaker photo)

The Volkswagen Kombi bus offered in ambulance trim was a factory conversion by the German automaker. This 1959 VW ambulance, originally operated by the Hatboro (Pa.) Fire Department, featured frosted glass (partial treatment) in the side windows as well as a choice of rear compartment interior plans as standard equipment and many were imported into North America. Larry Holbert of Pennsylvania is the owner of this vehicle. (Old Cars photo)

Chevrolet trucks also saw ambulance duty with the 1963 Series 10 Suburban outfitted for emergency work. Dual spotlights were part of the equipment package. (Old Cars photo)

Barely visible on this 1965 Cadillac ambulance is the alarm siren mounted up front behind the grille. Highly noticeable are the dual tunnel-type roof-mounted marker lights front and rear, dual spotlights and dual fender-mounted warning lights. Also note the deeply tinted windshield. (Old Cars photo)

Kaiser-Jeep Corp. offered an ambulance conversion on its 1966 Jeep J-100 four-wheel-drive Wagoneer. Note that this unit has right-hand drive marking this as an export model. Also note the rear windows are frosted and not because of the cold weather. (Kaiser-Jeep photo)

Recovery is anything but routine...

The well-worn phrase "It's a dirty job, but someone has to do it," might have been originated decades ago by a tow truck operator hooking up to a car that on some cold, rainy night slid out of control and landed upside down in a muddy ditch. Almost since the day automobiles started journeying from point A to point B, there has been a need for recovery vehicles. The earliest rigs were dispatched to recover motorcars stuck hub deep in mud or stopped and tilting awkwardly due to broken wheel spokes or literally scattered in pieces after an accident.

Controversy exists as to who manufactured the first "recovery" vehicle, loosely identified as such because at its origin the "tow truck" was more commonly referred to as a wrecking crane or auto crane (see the ads on the following pages). This is due to the fact that, unlike modern rigs built specifically for towing or hauling duty, early recovery vehicles used a crane boom that was affixed to the frame of a truck or bed of a pickup or even to a larger, touring-type automobile modified to accept this equipment. Other publications and even a museum (International Towing & Recovery Hall of Fame and Museum, 401 Broad St., Chattanooga, TN 37402, ph. 423-267-3132) exist that delve into the fascinating history of tow trucks. The towing vehicles that are pictured throughout this book are presented to show how they have both evolved and served through the years at the accident scene.

Many of the accidents depicted in this book involved what could be termed as a "routine" recovery. This simply means the front or back of the damaged vehicle was hoisted off the ground and it was then towed back to the body shop or dealership for repair. But in an equal number of accidents shown, the challenge — and often times risk — to the tow truck operator performing his duty is evident in the aftermath of a particularly grinding crash or an accident where the damaged vehicle ended up wrapped around a power pole or any other number of strange scenarios that tow truck operators face regularly at accident scenes. A few such scenarios found in this book include the wrecker operator trying to "tow" a dump truck out from a clump of trees, minus one of its front wheels. The tow truck is pictured doing a "wheelie" as it appears unable to move the disabled dump truck, so the operator has a few men pile on the hood of the tow truck for ballast. From the comical to the potentially life threatening was the accident scene where a car was driven off a California cliff. The tow truck operator had to climb down the cliff with tow cable in-hand to attach it to the damaged car. In that recovery, the tow cable and hook doubled as a rappeler's life line.

So, while doing wheelies and rock climbing may not be common activities for the tow truck operator, there is no "routine" when it comes to recovering a vehicle that has come to rest in an unusual position or place after a crash has occurred. While looking at some of the badly mangled vehicles in this book, imagine what the tow truck operator had to do to clear the accident scene in a safe and timely manner — many times doing his job in front of a crowd of onlookers, with shattered glass and/or spilled gasoline or lubricant underfoot. And in many cases, where smaller towns were concerned, responding to an accident scene where the tow truck operator may have known the people involved in the crash, whether they were injury victims or fatalities. Not always (ever?) a pleasant job to be sure, but one that has a professional respond when recovery duty calls.

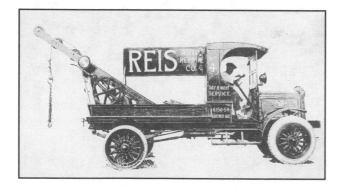

Eagle Model 105 three-ton garage service truck. This 1920s rig, operated by the Reis Auto Repair Co., of St. Louis, had a crane capacity of 22,000 pounds. Note the hard rubber tires in the rear and balloon tires mounted in front. (Minette Reis Grunik Bethke photo)

The original photo is too fuzzy to identify the tow truck, but its operator used a system of cable, pulley and sling to retrieve a mid-1930s Chevrolet cab and chassis (possibly the rest of the truck was lost during its descent) from the bottom of a rocky drop-off. Early recovery vehicles, as well as their operators, had to be able to work in all weather conditions and often in dangerous situations due to poor road conditions. (Coy Thomas photo)

"Jesse can pull it out"

Jesse F. Gregg Jr., of Rio Grande, N.J., writes: "The 1954 Ford F600 wrecker in the picture had an engine from an AF800 bus. The wrecker was owned and operated by my father, Jesse F. Gregg Sr., from 1959 until his death in 1982.

"The wrecking boom was originally installed on a cut-down Buick-built Marquette, and was hand-cranked only. It was constructed entirely by my father. In 1947 or 1948 the boom was put on a 1940 Ford, with the winch at the rear off the power takeoff through a Model A Ford transmission to gear it down. The winch was off an army truck, the wing at the rear was a dead man, lowered down with the winch until it went into the ground about six or seven inches.

After backing up on it about two feet, there was nothing it wouldn't pull out.

"Possibly it was the most powerful wrecker on the eastern shore of Maryland! It was known to have pulled out fertilizer trucks stuck down to their frames. The saying was: 'If Jesse can get to it, he can pull it out.' Vehicles that were pulled out by this tow truck included: feed trucks, soil service trucks, gas trucks, firetrucks, poultry trucks and, on two occasions, bulldozers."

Possibly the most powerful tow truck on the eastern shore of Maryland between 1959 and 1982 was Jesse Gregg Sr.'s 1954 Ford F600. (Jesse F. Gregg Jr. photo)

Making the grade

M.E. "Red" Burke of Fort Bragg, Calif., writes: "The 1930 Model A Ford roadster crashed in 1937 on a twisting mountainous road between Fillmore and Moorpark (California) that we called Grimes Canyon Road. I'm the young man on the left in the white coveralls. The other man leaning on the shovel handle is Harry Wileman, the father of one of my co-workers at Rudkin Motor Service (DeSoto-Plymouth) for whom I worked for 17 years.

"The wrecker (behind the Ford) we built from a 1926 Lincoln touring car taken in trade from a local ranch owner. The Ford roadster had gone off a sharp curve and tumbled many times into a ravine below. Both men in the car were thrown out and killed. It turned out later that they had stolen the car in North Hollywood and were desperate to get out of the Los Angeles area.

"We got the call from the California Highway Patrol to remove the Ford from the ravine. I drove up the grade and finally found the car and saw that I wouldn't be able to retrieve it with the old Lincoln, which had a hand-crank Manley wrecking crane with one cable of 150-foot length. So I got Harry Wileman to load his International T20 tractor on his trailer behind his 1932 Ford Model BB truck and come help.

"We put the tractor on the edge of the road crossways. We then hooked all the cables and chains together and pulled across the road, unhooked and shortened up the chains, and repeated this process until we had that Ford up on the road. We then had to winch it onto Harry's trailer to bring it to Fillmore. There was no part of this car that was salvageable. It sat in a lean-to shed behind Rudkin's used car lot for several years. Incidentally, the Lincoln wrecker was replaced by one we built out of a 1933 Lincoln limousine. Actually, neither one was suitable for a wrecker."

"Red" Burke (left) and Harry Wileman pose with the 1930 Ford roadster that they recovered from the bottom of a ravine off Grimes Canyon Road in California in 1937. (M.E. "Red" Burke photo)

The Auto Wrecking Crane Was Originated by Robert E. Manley in 1917

The Manley Crane was the first automobile wrecking crane to be manufactured and offered to dealers and garage men of this country.

Watch for Manley Cranes on the road. You will notice that "The Manleys" predominate wherever you go.

The tremendous number of satisfied users is the best argument in favor of the Manley Crane.

MECHANICALLY CORRECT
NOTE THESE MANLEY FEATURES

SWIVEL NOSE which permits direct pull from any angle.

TILTING BEAM (*originated by Manley*) permits adjustment of height and overhang to suit various conditions.

DOUBLE HANDLES can be operated from either side of car.

SIX LEVERAGES AND SPEEDS so that crane can be operated easily on different loads.

CHAIN OR CABLE furnished at your option, but we recommend the chain.

SELF CONTAINED SADDLE (*originated by Manley*) distributes weight properly on chassis, yet base occupies minimum amount of space.

ONLY TWO GEARS. The use of high ratio gearing employing only two gears, eliminates unnecessary friction which results from compounding the gearing.

EXCESS STRENGTH. Like all Manley equipment, the cranes are built with strength away beyond their rated capacity.

Get a Manley

Manley Jobbers Everywhere Can Supply You.

MANLEY MFG. CO., YORK, PA.

Ad touting Manley Crane from 1925 *Motor Age* magazine. (Old Cars photo)

Your Greatest ASSET!

HOLMES WRECKER No. 485

The Holmes Wrecker No. 485 will earn greater dividends per dollar invested than any other equipment the repair shop or service station can operate. Hardly a day passes even in the smallest community that some serious motor mishap does not create a profitable, open-price repair job for the Holmes Equipped shop.

From the simplest towing job to the most difficult wreck, this equipment is supreme, handling every situation with speed, ease and with absolutely no further damage to the wrecked car.

Motorists are quick to appreciate the efficiency of the Holmes No. 485. When it passes through the streets, or when they see it in operation, they immediately recognize that your equipment is up to date. When trouble comes to them they naturally call you knowing you can handle their difficulties with speed, safety and economy. The towing fees alone from these calls pay for your Holmes Wrecker in a few weeks time.

Your jobber will be glad to show you some of the records of profits Holmes Wreckers have made. Or, if you will write the factory, complete information will be mailed at once.

ERNEST HOLMES COMPANY

CHATTANOOGA   TENNESEE

HOLMES GARAGE PRESS

Nothing can so reduce your labor costs as this combination Arbor and Heavy Duty Garage Press. It leads the field in speed, efficiency and convenience.

The bolster is quickly adjusted to any height by means of a simple, self-contained hoisting mechanism. The high speed lever has a thrust capacity of 4,000 pounds, while the low speed spike wheel exerts a powerful pressure of 60,000 pounds. All strokes are downward and all levers are right-hand operated. Two casters mounted on the frame permit the press to be rolled about the shop.

HOLMES CANTILEVER JACK

This rugged jack embodies all the desirable features of the most efficient equipment on the market. It can raise or lower its load from any position with any length stroke, and has a lifting range of from 6 to 17 inches, making it universal for all cars.

It is just as simple to lower as it is to raise. No load on handle when lowering. No pawls or levers to operate.

Ad promoting Holmes Wrecker #485 from 1927 *Motor Age* magazine. (Old Cars photo)

The profits are big from bringing home the cripples

Wrecking and towing—man, the *profits* they bring. Not only towing them home, but the service work *after* they're home.

The Weaver Crane was produced with the advice of hundreds of garage men who know what a crane *must have*—how strong it must be—what work it must *do*.

It is light in weight—but husky *and speedy* in performance. 4000 pounds are easy for *this* crane. Takes only small space on a truck, leaving plenty of room for equipment, and one man can handle an entire wrecking job.

It's the biggest profit maker you can put on your payroll. *Put it on.*

Weaver Mfg. Co.
Springfield, Ill., U.S.A.

**Weaver Canadian Co., Ltd.
Chatham, Ontario**

Literature that describes it? You bet! Just send a post card

WEAVER
AUTO CRANE

Lower Shaft permits quick adjustment of the chains to the load. For maximum power in lifting the load, upper shaft is used.

The Swivel Head prevents any binding of the chain when pull is from one side.

Ask your Jobber's Salesman he's a WEAVER salesman too!

ADV. PICARD-SOHN, INC., N. Y.

The Weaver Auto Crane is exhibited in this mid-1920s ad from *Automobile Trade Journal*. (Old Cars photo)

At the time when the wrecker originated, it was often referred to as a service car even though most were based on trucks with aftermarket crane units (usually rated at 4,000-6,000 pounds) attached to their beds. "Smiley," the tow truck driver for Williamson Motor Co., is at the wheel of a 1929 Ford Model AA. (Old Cars photo)

Along with gas, oil and cold drinks, "Chic" Scheible's filling station in Florida circa 1913 offered triple A towing service on the hook of a Buick touring car modified for wrecker service. Note the visible, gravity flow gas pumps under the pagoda-style shelters. (Old Cars photo courtesy of the Strozier Archives of Florida State University)

This restored, modified 1934 Ford V-8 truck utilizing a Weaver Auto Crane was offered for sale at a 1980s auction. (Old Cars photo)

M and E Auto Body Works of Kansas City, Kan., used this beautiful 1935 Diamond T one-ton wrecker in its business. Note the roof-mounted spotlight for the nighttime portion of "24-hour service." (Joe Egle photo)

This restored 1936 Dodge tow truck was photographed while on display at Hershey, Pa., in 1987. Note the small toolbox located on the runningboard. (Old Cars photo)

The Car Farm of Wild Rose, Wis., operates this early-1940s Chevrolet wrecker with modified exhaust stack. (Old Cars photo)

What better vehicle to withstand the rigors of wrecker service than a Dodge Power Wagon! This 1946 unit saw heavy usage while operated as part of South Leeds Garage in Deforest, Wis. The four-wheeled towing dolly attached to the boom could be used under the wheels of the non-hooked end of a vehicle in a situation where the entire vehicle had to be off the ground while towing. (Old Cars photo)

The cab and chassis of a 1949 Nash was the base for this restored tow truck owned by Ken Havekost of Ken's Nash Motors collector vehicle business in Monroe, Mich. (Old Cars photo)

Irv Hall was proud of his new Dodge tow truck and photographed it in a park in the late 1940s near his Wausau, Wis., garage business. Note the convenient step pads mounted above the runningboard and rear fender to allow access to the boom and equipment stored in the bed. (Robert Dalsky photo)

The Hall Dodge wrecker in action pulling a 1951 Packard back onto the road after it crashed through a section of post and cable on an icy Wisconsin roadway in 1952. (Robert Dalsky photo)

A 1951 Diamond T 420 tow truck in the service of the Washington, D.C. Metropolitan Police Department drives near the U.S. Capitol building in search of parking violators' illegally parked cars. Note the "no parking" sign in the background. (Old Cars photo)

George Kaiser of Pennsylvania is the owner of this restored 1953 Ford F-500 wrecker, which was photographed while on display at Hershey, Pa., in 1990. (Old Cars photo)

Even the light-duty Willys Jeep of the mid-1950s saw service as a tow vehicle. The large photo shows the Jeep's undercarriage towing sling set up to be attached to lift a disabled car, with the car's bumper resting against the rubber pads to prevent scratches. (Inset) The Jeep with the towing boom neatly stowed between jobs. (Old Cars photos)

Manley used a late-1950s Chevrolet Apache Series 3600 Fleetside 3/4-ton pickup to promote its WC-3 wrecker unit with extendible boom. (Old Cars photo)

The 1965 Dodge D-500 could be outfitted for wrecker service, including a 15,000-pound load capacity, two-speed rear axle and dual rear wheels. The bed and wrecker boom are Ashton products. As tradition goes, this tow truck is named "Miss Julie." (Old Cars photo)

A 1967 Ford Bronco outfitted as a tow truck, but using the opposite end to push start a stalled station wagon. (Old Cars photo)

At the front of this section there was an ad promoting Holmes' wrecker #485 from 1927. Forty-five years later, in 1972, Ford promoted its F350 Ranger truck using a Holmes Model 500 wrecker boom. Note on the bed was stenciled "Since 1916" indicating the longevity of the Ernest Holmes Co. (Old Cars photo)

"In the view of some of the press, the automobile is today a juggernaut, a motoring speed-monster, intent on killing and maiming all who stand in its way. The motorist ... is an intoxicated savage, in charge of a dangerous device."
"The Romance of the Automobile Industry" - 1916
James R. Doolittle (quoted in ***The Struggle for Auto Safety*** - 1990
Jerry L. Mashaw and David L. Harfst)

On the road to ruin . . .

While the scenery is breathtaking in this mid-1920s photograph of a Canadian highway, it perfectly points out the dangers inherent in early motoring. Roads were rough, rutted lanes gouged out of the earth. The wood railing pictured would not keep a vehicle from breaking through and plunging downhill, with dire consequences. Accidents were often caused by vehicle malfunctions, which, in turn, were caused by these primitive road conditions. Splintered wood spoke wheels and flat tires were as common as the dirt they rode on. But just as often, accidents were caused by driver error: Speeding, inattentiveness and driving while intoxicated caused needless suffering then and still does to this day. The hundreds of photos that follow are a reminder that even though the primitive road conditions were eventually eliminated by thousands of miles of paved, level stretches of well-lit, well-marked roadways, accidents caused by driver carelessness remain a black mark on our society. (Old Cars photo)

Harold McAdam of Ogdensburg, N.Y., writes: "This is my grandfather's 1907 Cadillac. The accident occurred on Route 68 just outside of Ogdensburg. The highway was being prepared for its first paving. The state had piled crushed stone along the side of the road. Grandfather drove up on one of these piles and rolled the Cadillac. He sustained a broken collarbone in the crash. Parts of the car were still on this farm after World War II. I still have the Cadillac's porcelain 1912 New York license plates and one headlight. Route 68 was paved in 1912. Grandfather always complained after that. He said he couldn't keep a horse shod on a road like that!" (Harold McAdam photo)

What this 1913 Hudson collided with is a mystery, but the result was its parts were scattered everywhere. The crash occurred in Waldo, Wis. Note the gas tank filler neck protruding from the dash. (Richard A. Williams photo)

One of the two Model T Fords involved in this broadside collision was torn in half with the back portion presumably ending up behind the crowd of people in the background. Note the hub odometer on the front wheel. (Ronald Marzlock photo)

According to his grandson, Ed Mehring was driving what appears to be a Studebaker with Iowa 1921 license plates, which was struck by a train. Aside from wheel problems, the car appears to have suffered little damage from the run-in. (Keith Kuehn photo)

Two views of what appears to be a mid-teens Overland touring involved in a sideswipe collision that damaged the rear wheel and fender. The license plate reads Massachusetts 1919. Note the splintered spoke wheel on the runningboard and the toolbox with its contents scattered about. (Old Cars photos)

A two-car crash in 1920 in Viroqua, Wis., occurred on Highway 27 and was caused by a drunk driver. A 1916 Model T (above) and an Oldsmobile (below) collided, with the Oldsmobile rolling over into a ditch. The Model T can be seen in the background behind the Olds. The tires were removed from the Olds to prevent their theft. (Larry C. Fjelsted photos)

A 1921 Cadillac touring with New Jersey 1930 license plates was wrecked in a roll-over accident. All the loose and broken parts loaded in the back suggest the car was towed from the accident scene and parked, awaiting its final journey to the scrap yard. (Ronald Marzlock photo)

According to his grandson, while trekking to Lake Tahoe in a 1918 Velie, Gunnar Anderson came upon this Cadillac that had tipped over. Anderson snapped a photo and placed it in a scrapbook with the caption "A mishap on the road." This angle offers a good view of the dual exhaust of the early V-8 engine Cadillac used. (Robert Fletcher photo)

Bill Lynch of Phoenix, Ariz., writes: "This wreck occurred in Seattle, Wash., in the early 1930s on a rainy night. My mother, Audrey Lynch, was driving and my father Gordon was a passenger in the 1928 Chevrolet roadster. The street was brick and the Chevy slid onto the tracks in the path of an oncoming street car. Immediately a street car traveling in the opposite direction also hit the car. Witnesses did not attempt to get my parents out of the car as they believed that no one could have survived the accident. My mother's nylons were in shreds, but there were no cuts on her legs. She only suffered a black eye. My dad sprained his wrist. He said that happened when he hit my mother! The Chevy was traded for the $7.00 tow bill." (Bill Lynch photo)

In 1937 in north Los Angeles, Calif., M.E. "Red" Burke was traveling on Riverside Drive when he witnessed a roll-over accident involving this 1929 Buick coupe that slid off the rain-slick highway. He remembers that no one was hurt, although a terrier dog inside the rear compartment was overcome from the fumes of spilled gasoline. The car was righted, suffering only minor damage, and the owner drove it away. (M.E. "Red" Burke photo)

> *Now the only way to lick a demon is not let him get the upper hand.*
> *Lose control of yourself and in steps the Rum Demon or the Dope Demon.*
> *Lose control of your car on a slippery street and old Demon Skid will take charge of the situation....*
> *And it's a bum driver that can't keep his car under control and prevent its skiddin'.*
> **Stay Alive** - 1928
> Marcus Dow speaking as Jim the Truckman

Already in the body shop for repair, this early series (still has drum headlights) 1928 Chandler received damage as a result of being tipped onto its side. The car has California 1931 license plates. Note the worn condition of the front tire. (Phil Evans photo)

Betty Broms Koets writes: "This is my father's friend Jack Nelson's family car that Jack was driving from Chicago to a north suburb to caddy on a Saturday morning in 1931. Jack was 17 years old and his mother was happy to let him use the car to earn money at the golf course. The car was a 1929 Oakland that was purchased new. While Jack was driving to the golf course, he was hit broadside by a Cadillac limousine, which knocked the body off the chassis. Jack walked away with a small cut on his cheek. He then telephoned his aunt and she went to his parent's home and told his mother, 'You lost your car, but your son is still here.'" (Betty Broms Koets photo)

Two of Buick's finest, a new 1934 sedan (left) and 1927 landau sedan (right), were destroyed in this head-on collision that occurred on New York's Northern State Parkway in 1934. Note the hubcap for the new Buick, which got knocked off and rolled undamaged under the car. (Ronald Marzlock photo)

Two of Chevrolet's finest, a new 1939 two-door sedan (left) and a late-1920s two-door sedan (right), were destroyed in this broadside collision that occurred in Iowa in 1939. The hood for the new Chevy ended up across the road in the ditch. (Dennis F. Hood photo)

A pair of Chevrolets, 1932 (wire wheels) and 1937 models, collided head-on at the corner of Cambridge and Mahoning Streets in Alliance, Ohio, in July of 1941. A tow truck can be seen in the background preparing to hook up to the older Chevy. (Frank A. Hoiles photo)

This double roll-over accident involved a 1931 Ford and an unidentified car on its side. (Bruce Craig photo)

It's safe to wait till others pass,
There ain't no doubt about it.
Tell that rule to a drivin' fool;
Don't whisper it, but shout it.
Stay Alive - 1928
Marcus Dow speaking as Jim the Truckman

Two views of a beautiful new 1931 Auburn convertible that received considerable front end and frame damage in a head-on collision in New York in 1931. Note the leather interior (below) and the "suicide" doors. Also shown (below) across the street is a Buick coupe. (Ronald Marzlock photo)

Don Ensch of Ventura, Calif., writes: "I purchased this 1924 Chevrolet Master Deluxe three-window coupe with rumbleseat as a returning serviceman in November 1946. It was my first car, and I paid $525 for it. It had 79,000 miles on the odometer. I drove it through my four years of college; it was a good runner and spiffy looker. At the time of the accident, it had run 110,000 miles. Sadly, on March 6, 1950, while driving the Pacific Coast Highway in Long Beach in dense fog, I was hit by a 1937 Ford. Both cars sustained major damage. My car was wrecked beyond its value. I sold the tires, then new, for $15 and the car for $10. Fortunately, no one was injured in the accident." (Don Ensch photos)

Robert Nickerson of Elk River, Minn., writes: "This photograph was taken in 1942 at Nickerson Bros. Garage (Ford and Mercury) in Elk River. The 1938 Ford lost to a freight train and was towed in by the garage's Ford wrecker. My father brought back many a wreck from where the cars lost out to trains halfway between Elk River and Big Lake ten miles to the northwest." (Robert Nickerson photo)

A 1935 Ford two-door sedan left the road and plowed through a wall in Middleton, N.Y., in 1948. (Marvin H. Cohen photo)

A true fender bender, this 1935 Chevrolet rear-ended another vehicle and got its front end rearranged. (Ronald Marzlock photo)

A 1936 Ford (background) collided with a 1938 Plymouth coupe at the intersection of Arch and South Streets in Alliance, Ohio, in October of 1940 with the Plymouth ending up against a power pole. A slick brick street may have contributed to the wreck. (Frank A. Hoiles photo)

William W. Nash of Friendsville, Pa., writes: "This bridge carried Conklin Avenue over Pierce Creek in Binghamton, N.Y. In the late 1930s, I was walking along Conklin about five blocks from home when I came upon this accident involving a 1937 Pontiac. I ran home and picked up the box camera we had and ran back to the accident scene. Instead of taking the picture from street level I climbed down into the creek bed. It was reported in the newspaper that the driver of the Pontiac had pulled out of Burr Avenue, an intersecting street, turned left onto Conklin but failed to straighten out and continued to make a 180-degree turn into the bridge railing. The railing was repaired with a solid one and for over 30 years the railings did not match." (William W. Nash photo)

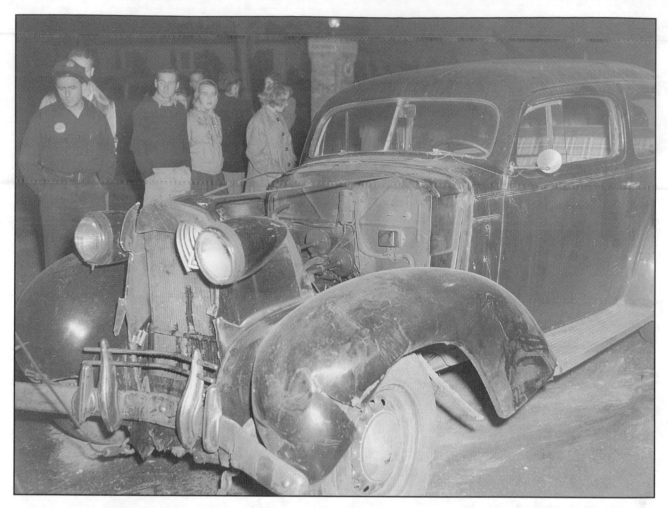

A crowd inspects the damage to a 1936 Oldsmobile that was involved in a head-on collision with another vehicle. Note the unusual tear in the fender caused by the crash. (Ronald Marzlock photo)

Kenny (in coveralls), an employee of Oscar's garage in Alliance, Ohio, unloads a 1936 Chevrolet coupe that was destroyed in a 1940 roll-over accident. (Frank A. Hoiles photo)

A wrecker operator stands next to the 1936 Chevrolet he would tow away from the accident scene after it was involved in a collision that damaged its front end. Even the far fender received a "dimple." (Ronald Marzlock photo)

What book would be complete without a celebrity tie-in, and the "Bambino" is up to bat as our very own celebrity wreck. On June 28, 1938, George Herman "Babe" Ruth collided with an oncoming car in Saddle River, N.J., and his 1936 Oldsmobile convertible coupe left the road. The Olds hit a brick wall and tipped over. According to the accident report, as he was helped from his damaged car Ruth said: 'Gosh, looks like I'll have to buy another one tomorrow.' The car was towed to a garage in Ramsey, N.J., where this photo was taken. (Ronald Marzlock photo)

A 1937 Plymouth "woodie" station wagon got its bumper torn off and fender crumpled in an accident in New York in 1951. This car was driven from the accident scene to its owner's home, with the front end alignment obviously out of whack. (Ronald Marzlock photos)

This 1937 Ford convertible rolled on its side in a 1950 crash in Massachusetts. Note the sealed beam headlight conversion kits on both the Ford and the 1939 Dodge in the background. (Charlie Harper photo)

Obviously the crowd around this wrecked 1937 Ford contains the store owners who appear happy the car came to rest on the sidewalk and didn't roll through the storefront windows and scatter the produce. (Ronald Marzlock photo)

A broadside collision at a New York residential intersection in 1950 slightly damaged this 1937 Plymouth coupe. The driver's door was wedged shut so the occupants had to exit through the passenger door. (Ronald Marzlock photo)

Onlookers inspect the 1937 Plymouth involved in a fender bender in Alliance, Ohio, in April of 1941. Note the radio antenna attached to the roof. (Frank A. Hoiles photo)

Already towed into Queen's Auto Service and Collision Work for repair, this 1937 Plymouth with Connecticut 1940 license plates was flattened a bit in a roll-over accident. In the lower photo, a V-12-powered Cadillac modified into a tow rig sits on jackstands in the background undergoing an overhaul. (Ronald Marzlock photos)

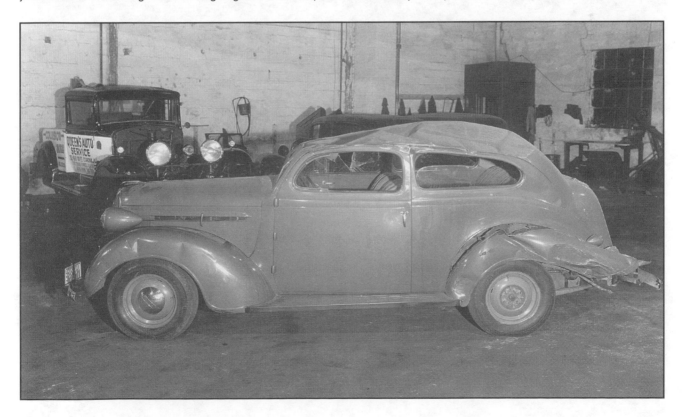

A government Chevrolet Suburban rear-ended a 1937 Pontiac, which in turn rear-ended a vehicle not shown in this chain reaction crash in Damascus, Ohio, in July of 1941. The Pontiac looks a mess with its bumper hanging down and headlight pods broken loose. (Frank A. Hoiles photo)

In a Buick dealership body shop awaiting repair, this 1938 Buick Special suffered a broadside impact that crushed the fender, bowed the runningboard and buckled the door. (Ronald Marzlock photo)

Two views of a 1938 Chevrolet that left the road and slammed into a power pole on Route 17 in Sullivan County, N.Y., in 1949. The tall white structure barely visible in the lower photo is a drive-in theater. (Marvin H. Cohen photos)

A minor collision at a crossroads must have injured a passenger who was being tended to inside this 1938 Chevrolet. The crowd in the background appears to contain the drivers of both vehicles involved in the crash who are discussing what happened. (Ronald Marzlock photo)

A snow covered road probably played a part in this head-on collision involving a 1938 Chevrolet sedan and a 1936 Chevy pickup operated by the Commonwealth Telephone Co. (Greg Holmes photo)

Of this multiple view accident scene David A. Johnson of West Kennebunk, Maine, writes: "This is a fender bender my dad was involved in around 1939. It occurred between Chester and Huntington, Mass., while he worked for a construction firm following the 1938 hurricane. It appears it was a tight squeeze on a snow covered road for my dad's 1938 Chevrolet (right) and the oncoming 1937 Dodge." (David A. Johnson photos)

What appears to be the remains of a 1941 car-train collision, this 1939 Dodge was towed to a New York salvage yard filled with interesting old tin by what can be seen in this shot. (Ronald Marzlock photo)

What this 1939 Chevrolet collided with is a mystery, but both the front and rear quarters of the car are damaged. Note the optional fog light on the bumper mount, which was a popular item on later Chevys (this accident occurred around 1950). (Ronald Marzlock photo)

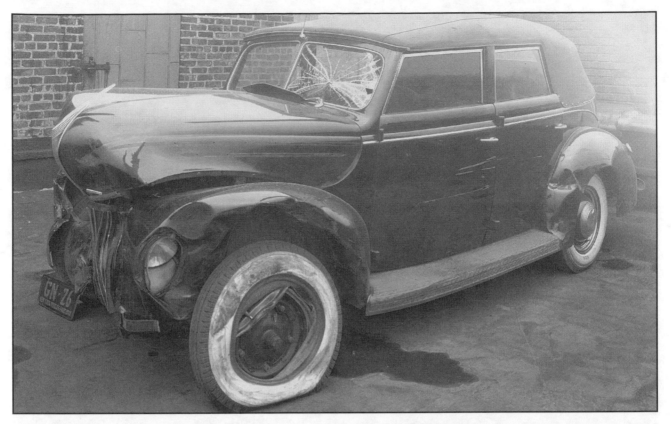

Only 3,561 1939 Ford DeLuxe convertible sedans were produced so it's extremely unfortunate this rare model got mangled in a head-on crash in New York in 1940. You can see the innertube sticking out from the bent lip of the front wheel (above). Note the huge Chevrolet billboard in the background (below). (Ronald Marzlock photos)

The look on the little girl's face peeking between the wrecked cars conveys the scene perfectly. A 1937 Lincoln Zephyr rear-ended a 1940 Chevrolet with the Lincoln worse off in the damage department. (Ronald Marzlock photo)

H.E. Johnston of Yates Center, Kan., writes: "This three car accident occurred in 1948 in Wilmington, Calif. I was driving the 1941 Chrysler New Yorker to work, when from the opposite direction a 1937 Willys came over the double yellow line to pass the 1936 Ford. We met head-on, and the Ford crashed into the two of us. Many injuries resulted to the driver of the Willys. This picture, taken by the Los Angeles Police Dept., was displayed at the downtown police station for many months and also appeared in the Auto Club of Southern California monthly newsletter." (H.E. Johnston photo)

The skid marks leading to the curb are barely visible on the brick street, and the gouge in the lawn explains why this late-1930s Plymouth tipped over on a residential Ohio sidewalk in 1950. Why the car skidded on dry pavement, though, remains a mystery, although excessive speed played a part in this accident. (Lloyd A. Himes photo)

A runaway truck not shown slammed into this row of vehicles in Liberty, N.Y., in 1948 creating a lot of business for the local body shop. The "squeeze job" involved (l-to-r) a 1939 Federal truck, eight-cylinder 1937 Oldsmobile, 1942 Plymouth, and 1947 Ford. (Marvin H. Cohen photo)

North Street in Middletown, N.Y., in 1951 was the scene of a two-car collision involving a 1939 Pontiac (left) and a 1949 Chevrolet. The white building in the background is a DeSoto-Plymouth dealership. (Marvin H. Cohen photo)

From the angle of this photo, the damage to the 1937 Chevrolet coupe (right) is not evident but it must have been severe if the amount of damage to the 1940 Buick convertible is any indication. This crash occurred in New Jersey in 1950. (Ronald Marzlock photo)

This 1940 Buick Special was involved in a sideswipe accident that flattened the passenger side of the car. Note that the impact was hard enough to dislodge the front coil spring. (Ronald Marzlock photo)

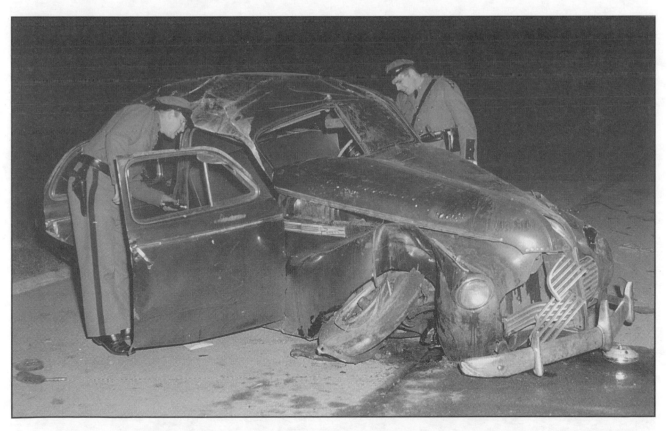

This 1940 Buick Super barrel rolled on the highway scattering parts and fluids everywhere. By the blistered paint on the hood the car appears to have caught fire in the engine compartment when it stopped flipping. Police officers inspect the interior looking for clues to help fill out the accident report. (Ronald Marzlock photo)

This 1941 Chevrolet had its front end peeled open in a crash on Route 17 near Middletown, N.Y., in 1948. It's been towed from the accident scene to a field. (Marvin H. Cohen photo)

Government vehicle #209, a 1941 Chevrolet Special Deluxe, was decommissioned due to a broadside crash. It was towed to a body shop, but appears to be too damaged to be anything but a parts donor candidate. (Phil Evans photo)

Lexington Road in Alliance, Ohio, in August of 1941 was the scene of this roll-over crash involving a 1940 Plymouth. The extent of the damage to the Plymouth was evident after the car was righted. (Frank A. Hoiles photo)

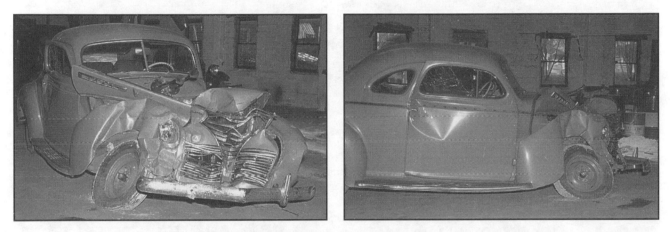

A mangled 1939 DeSoto involved in a 1941 head-on collision in Alliance, Ohio, awaits salvaging after it was towed from the accident scene to a body shop. (Frank A. Hoiles photo)

Not much remains of the sheet metal to identify this 1941 Ford coupe that got peeled open in a collision with something big such as a train or truck. It almost appears that if the tires were aired up, the car could be driven away. (Charlie Harper photo)

The tow truck operator sitting on the cowl of this 1941 Chevrolet earned his pay retrieving this car. The Chevy rolled down a cliff to the right and the tow truck had to have its rear wheels chocked while the cables visible on the ground were walked down the cliff and attached to the car so it could be winched back to level ground. There is another tow truck barely visible in the background, and both might have been needed to retrieve the Chevy. (Phil Evans photo)

Nothing more sad to see than a shiny new car get mashed in a wreck, but that's exactly what happened to this 1941 Oldsmobile in Alliance, Ohio, in August of 1941. The crash occurred on South Union Street where the car was hooked up to a wrecker to be towed to the dealership for repair. (Frank A. Hoiles photo)

Both the front wheel and rear axle of this 1941 Buick Super convertible were torn off in a grinding sideswipe collision with another vehicle. The accident occurred in Massachusetts in the 1950s. (Charlie Harper photo)

This 1941 Buick Super convertible came to a "full stop," although on the wrong side of the road, due to two flat tires. The scraping along the side of the car suggests a brush against something low such as fencing or a fire hydrant. (Ronald Marzlock photo)

The tow truck is already at the scene of this glancing head-on collision with a roadside tree involving a 1941 Buick Super convertible sedan. Note the twig on the hood and the broken branch under the driver's door, suggesting the tree was as beat up as the car. (Ronald Marzlock photo)

Amazingly, that's the car's passenger door wrapped around the light standard at right. This 1941 Buick Special was pretty rusted out prior to being involved in this crash, suggesting a high-mileage older car that burned oil if the crushed motor oil can on the sidewalk is any indication. A tow truck is just visible over the roof and the wrecker operator is looking how best to hook up to the Buick to tow it off the sidewalk. (Ronald Marzlock photo)

This 1941 Chevrolet Special Deluxe rolled over into a tree, which crushed the driver's compartment. A police officer (below) using a flashlight inspects the accident scene. (Ronald Marzlock photo)

New York in 1951 was the scene of this roll-over accident involving a 1941 Chevrolet Master Deluxe. The question is, was the car towed or driven from the accident scene to this streetside location? While it appears the car was intact enough to drive, the chain just visible (above) protruding from the rear frame suggests it was towed. (Ronald Marzlock photo)

Accessorized to the hilt with foglights, fender guides, spotlight, fender porthole trim, antenna streamer, vent visor, and more, this 1942 Chevrolet Special Deluxe has a dented fender and hood. The hat on the fender suggests the car may have run into a pedestrian. Whatever happened, the accident took place in New York in 1948. (Ronald Marzlock photo)

This 1946 Chevrolet rolled over and slammed into a tree in North Ridgeville, Ohio. The car was bent so severely that the center of the frame touched the ground and held the passenger side front wheel off the ground. (Robert Gilder photo)

According to Kenneth J. Acord of Long Beach, Calif., this wreck took place in the 1940s on Cherry Avenue near the Pacific Coast Highway in Long Beach. The 1942 Chevrolet is a police car. Note the blackout trim and wartime license plates. The interior shot shows the dashboard was buckled, probably by a police officer's knee. The front wheel broke off on impact with its center section still attached to the brake drum. The brick building in the background still exists, according to Mr. Acord. (Kenneth J. Acord photos)

The driver of this 1947 Hudson Commodore Six has that "this-can't-be-happening-to-me" look after crunching a fender and losing the door trim piece in an accident. (Ronald Marzlock photo)

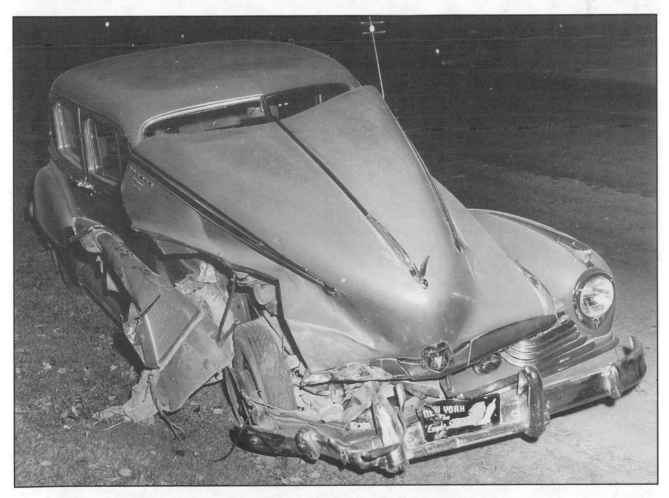

A 1947 Hudson Commodore Eight clipped another vehicle while traveling in New York and its front end got smashed. Note the aftermarket radio reception "booster" mounted on the antenna. (Ronald Marzlock photo)

The side of this 1947 Buick convertible got chewed up in a sideswipe accident that occurred in New York in 1950. The piece in the road (below) is the fender skirt, which got doubled up in the crash. (Ronald Marzlock photos)

The little boy peering out the window of this 1947 Chevrolet Stylemaster appears to be a bit scared (or camera-shy) after the car he was riding in was involved in a fender bender in a residential area of New York. The front tire was blown out in the crash and had to be changed. (Ronald Marzlock photo)

Upon close examination of this 1947 Dodge coupe it's evident that both sides of the car received extensive damage in what could have been a multiple car collision. Note the wheel trim rings that give the appearance of whitewall tires. (Ronald Marzlock photo)

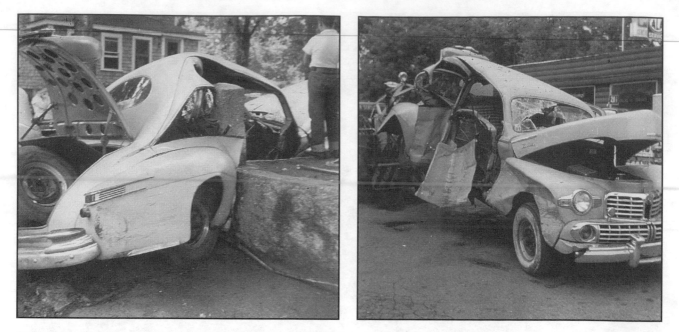

The stone block this 1948 Lincoln slammed into in Holliston, Mass., in 1955 absolutely crushed the midsection of the luxury car. The outer door sheet metal has been ripped away from its inner framework in the crash. (Charlie Harper photos)

The two cars involved in a glancing head-on collision on Route 17 in Middletown, N.Y., in 1949 have been moved from the accident scene to a nearby field. The cars involved were a 1941 Buick (left) and a 1948 Cadillac convertible. (Marvin H. Cohen photo)

There was a third car (or more) not pictured involved in this crash as the 1947 Oldsmobile (left) has major damage to its side not inflicted by the 1948 Ford that has rear-ended it. The collision occurred on Route 17 near Middletown, N.Y., circa 1950. (Marvin H. Cohen photo)

This late-1940s Ford was flattened in a roll-over crash in Middletown, N.Y., circa 1950. It was towed from the accident scene to a local garage for possible rebuilding. (Marvin H. Cohen photo)

How ironic that the Kansas City (Missouri) Police Dept.'s 1948 Ford accident investigation squad car would itself be involved in a crash. On the trunk lid is painted "Drive Slow" and the megaphone bolted to the Ford's roof was probably used to relay safety messages to the public. Note the new 1949 Lincoln in the dealer showroom in the background. (William K. Miller photo)

This roll-over accident involving a 1948 Packard occurred in June of 1952. The car flipped so hard its roof was flattened over the driver's compartment. (Peter Kanze photo)

> *Automobiles, by contrast, rapidly became the leading source of accidental death, injury, and property damage in the United States. Within 25 years of the first known automobile fatality, motor vehicle mishaps became the nation's leading cause of accidental death. And for every person fatally injured in a motor vehicle accident, an additional 35 people sustained nonfatal injuries.*
>
> "Motor Vehicle Accidents" - 1933
> from the ***Encyclopedia of Social Science***
> (quoted in ***The Struggle for Auto Safety*** - 1990
> Jerry L. Mashaw and David L. Harfst)

A two-car collision at a residential intersection on a rain-soaked street demolished the front end of this 1948 Chrysler Town & Country. The other vehicle is not shown, but the amount of damage it suffered must have been great if this Chrysler is any indication. The spare tire is out to replace the flat front tire, probably to make the tow truck operator's job a little easier. (Ronald Marzlock photo)

Howard V. Scotland Jr. of Cheyenne, Wyo., writes: "These two pictures are of my father's 1948 Buick Roadmaster convertible, which I was driving one Sunday night in April of 1949. While rounding a downhill curve on a wet road that had recently been resurfaced with tar and loose gravel, I lost control of the car, slid off the road, clipped a telephone pole and came to rest against a concrete culvert. As you can see by the photos, the car was a total loss, but the six occupants were relatively unhurt. This group of teenagers was a rather indestructible lot as witnessed by the fact that it was my face that did the damage to the driver's side windshield and my left shoulder that sprung the driver's door away from the frame. The Buick had 3,000 miles on the odometer at the time of the accident." (Howard V. Scotland Jr. photos)

Two views of a crumpled 1948 Oldsmobile 98 convertible that crashed in a residential area with much new construction going on. The damage appears to be mostly cosmetic, and this Olds 98, with fewer than 13,000 convertibles produced in 1948, was a sure candidate for repair. The police (above) and a tow truck (below) have arrived for the post-accident investigation and clean-up. (Ronald Marzlock photos)

This 1948 Studebaker Champion convertible appears to have rear-ended another vehicle at some other location and was then driven and parked on this, the street of giant trees and shrub walls. Fewer than 10,000 1948 Champion convertibles were built so this car was a probable project for the local body shop. (Ronald Marzlock photo)

The young man in the photo obviously finds humor in the fact that this 1948 Dodge came to rest against a "Thru Traffic Stop" sign as well as a tree after being hit by another vehicle (not shown) in the fender area. The car was relatively new as this accident occurred in New York in 1948. Police officers investigating the crash are barely visible in the background. (Ronald Marzlock photo)

Look close and the damage to the fender skirt and rear fender becomes evident on this 1948 Buick Roadmaster convertible. The trench-like tire marks behind the rear wheels are a mystery unless the Buick was backed into this position. Note the New York 1954 Pontiac Chieftan Special police car just ahead of the Buick. (Ronald Marzlock photo)

This little 1948 Crosley got even smaller after a run-in with another vehicle in 1950. The car was towed to this field in Middletown, N.Y., after the accident. (Marvin H. Cohen photo)

No problem driving this wrecked 1948 Chevrolet Fleetmaster to drop off some dry cleaning at Peter's 24-hour shop, and waiting until the local body shop has the time to make repairs. (Ronald Marzlock photo)

Although this crash doesn't appear to be that serious, if you have an accident the best place for it would be next to a hospital (background). A little bodywork and a radiator patch job and this new 1948 Studebaker Commander Starlight coupe looked new again. (Ronald Marzlock photo)

Robert R. Johnson of Minneapolis, Minn., writes: "This is a photo of my 1949 Pontiac convertible after a car filled with college students hit it while it was parked in St. Peter, Minn. It happened in the spring of 1951. It cost $900 to get the car fixed and I drove it until 1955. It would be nice if I still had it today." Note the Cities Service sign in the background. (Robert R. Johnson photo)

This 2200 Series (early) 1949 Packard "woodie" station sedan was already "getting the hook" from a tow truck operator (in back) after being involved in a frontal collision. Presumably the hood would not latch properly due to the damage and was removed for towing purposes. (Ronald Marzlock photo)

A 1949 Chevrolet Deluxe convertible with aftermarket "leopard skin" upholstery, presumably driven by one of the young chefs standing nearby talking to the representative of Bob's Auto Parts, received front end damage in a crash across the street from Ann's Tavern In New York. (Ronald Marzlock photo)

Most of the debris on the ground in front of this 1949 Chevrolet Deluxe came from whatever vehicle this Chevy collided with. The accident occurred in New York in 1960. Note the accessory "Buick" portholes mounted on the Chevy's front fender. The bumper guard by the front tire would also appear to be from the other vehicle. (Ronald Marzlock photo)

What this 1949 Kaiser Traveler collided with that would have caused such spotty damage is a mystery. Barely visible above the dent in the hood is a hood ornament not introduced on Kaisers until 1951, and further modified on this car with the addition of what appears to be a Dodge ram ornament affixed to the top of the non-stock Kaiser unit. (Ronald Marzlock photo)

According to Larry C. Fjelsted of Cassville, Wis., "The race for the railroad crossing was a tie, but the train won." The 1949 Oldsmobile 88 had its front end torn off in the 1950 collision that occurred on Highway 133 south of Cassville. The truck hauling milk cans is a late-1940s Chevrolet. The cars are a 1939 Plymouth (left) and 1941 Chevy. (Larry C. Fjelsted photo)

According to Norman Veness of Savage, Minn., this 1949 Buick Super convertible was his first car. In 1953, because of "too little sleep and one too many beers," he went off the road and hit a driveway in Bloomington, Minn. The car was repaired. (Norman Veness photo)

The roots of the tree knocked over are sticking out from underneath this 1949 Buick Super convertible that left the road and ended up on someone's front lawn. Luckily, the birdhouse was in the next tree over. (Ronald Marzlock photo)

It is ironic how two totally different accidents can be so similar, but that's the case with these two 1949 Ford "tudor" models. Both were involved in head-on collisions in New York. In both cars the steering columns collapsed causing the steering wheels to "lift" straight up. The buckling of the cars' hoods is almost identical. And, sadly, both crashes caused loss of life. (top - Peter Kanze photo/bottom - Ronald Marzlock photo)

The fender-mounted dual air horns on this 1949 Lincoln look big enough to blast the power pole out of the way but that didn't happen in this crash, which occurred in Kansas City, Mo., in 1951. The Lincoln was "dressed up" with a sun visor, vent visors, spotlights, gravel guards, antenna-mounted radio reception booster and fender trim from a 1951 Lincoln. Several of K.C.'s finest were at the scene investigating the accident. (William K. Miller photo)

This wreck involving what appears to be a mid-1950s International pickup that was rammed broadside by a 1946 Cadillac and then tipped over really drew a crowd. It's unusual with a police officer on-hand that he would allow people to get so close to what appears to be a pool of gasoline on the ground around the front of the truck. From this angle the Cadillac doesn't appear too damaged for the severity of the crash. (Stephen R. Behling photo)

A 1950 Chevrolet Deluxe rammed a late-1940s Dodge pickup broadside causing the truck to overturn. The accident occurred in Ohio in 1958. It appears as if both the roof and back window of the Chevy have either been painted or were coated with dirt, possibly from the crash. (Lloyd A. Himes photo)

An early-1950s Chevrolet truck hit a 1949 Plymouth broadside in Marshall, Mich., in 1954. The Ford that's barely visible behind the accident scene is a police car. (Milt Jenks photo)

Two views of a 1950 Dodge Wayfarer that slammed into a tree. No less than five police officers responded to this crash (below) and just visible behind the cops is a 1957 Plymouth police car. (Ronald Marzlock photos)

A late-1950s GMC tow truck has already lifted this wrecked 1950 Dodge to take it from the accident scene. A 1959 Plymouth police car was also present. The Dodge's add-on bumper guard didn't hold up too well. (Ronald Marzlock photo)

Whatever this 1950 Ford convertible had a run-in with destroyed the car, to the point of shearing off the carburetor and air filter canister from the top of the engine and peeling back the ragtop. The crash happened in 1954. (Peter Kanze photo)

Aside from a flat tire and a wrinkled rear fender, this 1950 Cadillac appears showroom-ready. This fender-bender happened in 1950 in New York. Note the Packard with the trunk-mounted emergency light in the background. (Ronald Marzlock photo)

This 1950 Oldsmobile 88 was sideswiped by another vehicle and basically peeled open, exposing the ventilation air duct behind the front fender. Note the bent lip of the front wheel and the fact that the bumper received no damage. It's a good bet the smiling young man is not the owner of the car! (Ronald Marzlock photo)

This accident scene looks similar to the one depicted on the front cover of this book, except this 1950 Pontiac drove onto a residential sidewalk in the daylight before hitting a power pole head-on. The Pontiac appears to be quite new, and was probably repaired. Note the policeman in the street directing traffic around the crash scene. (Ronald Marzlock photo)

The railroad tracks in the background are a good indication of what happened to this 1951 Buick, which appears to have almost been cut in two pieces. The crash occurred in Maryland in 1958. (Lawrence J. Gaddis/Martin L. Best photo)

A head-on collision on Michigan Avenue in Marshall, Mich., in 1954 involved a 1951 Ford Custom and a 1950 Cadillac. A late-1940s Dodge tow truck (below) from Connie's garage is backed up to the Cadillac to hook on while a police officer in the street directs traffic away from the accident scene. The Ford has snow tires mounted on the front. Note the "OK" used car sign (above) in the car lot across the street. (Milt Jenks photos)

Two young ladies examine the wreckage of a 1951 Chevrolet convertible that collided head-on with a tree in Middletown, N.Y., circa 1950. (Marvin H. Cohen photo)

Towed from the accident scene and propped up on a brick in a lot at the Waldo (Wis.) Service Garage, this is what remained of a new 1951 Oldsmobile convertible involved in a head-on crash. (Richard A. Williams photo)

Possibly wrecked while out on a test drive, this 1951 Cadillac had 1959 Maryland dealer license plates. The pieces of shrubbery visible on the antenna and fender corner suggest the car left the road. The headlight rim that remained undamaged appears to be from a 1952 Cadillac. (Lawrence J. Gaddis/Martin L. Best photo)

John J. Marvel of Hoyt Lakes, Minn., submitted this photo with a title: 1951 Frazer After Mom Did It In. He writes: "In the spring of 1957 in Meadowlands, Minn., my mother was driving on a gravel, rutted, frost-damaged road and lost control. The Frazer went square into a ditch. The car was totaled. She was unhurt." (John J. Marvel photo)

A 1951 Ford Custom Deluxe named "Linda" acquired a few wrinkles in a broadside collision in New York in 1958. Linda was wearing a few accessories such as aftermarket wings on the hood badge and the trim to make the car appear to be a Crestliner. Wet road conditions may have been a factor in the crash. (Ronald Marzlock photo)

While the "mid-century Mercs" are a favorite of modern customizers, this 1951 Mercury got its bodywork rearranged in a crash in New York in 1960. What appears to be a Ford tow truck was at the accident scene to remove the Merc. (Ronald Marzlock photo)

The front of this 1951 Pontiac got bent in a two vehicle collision in New York in 1960. A police officer at the accident scene took statements from what appear to be the two drivers involved. The Cadillac in the background may have been the second car in the accident. (Ronald Marzlock photo)

The tow truck boom is just visible over the front of this smashed 1951 Buick, which was involved in a crash in New York in 1960. The damaged hood was probably removed from the car to keep it from flying up while the Buick was being towed. Note the unusual pattern of destruction to only half the windshield. (Ronald Marzlock photo)

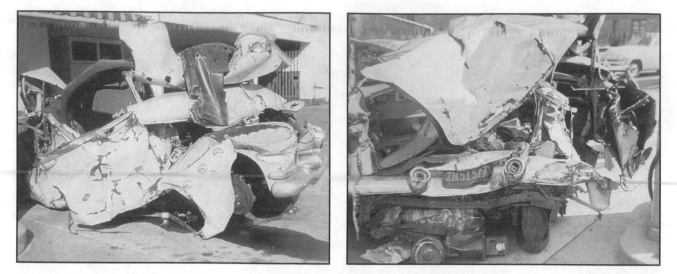

Herbert Michels of Midland, Mich., writes: "This 1951 Buick convertible was on its way to a filling station to get gas and was hit by a train. I took these pictures when I was in the military stationed in California in 1952. Fortunately the Buick's driver walked away from the accident." In the left photo, the driver's side fender and inner fender are piled on the hood of the car. The photo at right is the rear view. Note the car's air cleaner underneath the crushed gas tank. (Herbert Michels photos)

Two views of a demolished 1951 Chrysler Town & Country Deluxe station wagon with 1952 South Carolina license plates, which took a hard shot in the rear from something large such as a train or bus. After the accident, the car was towed to Polley Motors in Middletown, N.Y. Note the jalopy stock car parked behind the Chrysler. (Marvin H. Cohen photos)

"*Accidents are primarily caused by attitude.... One cure for accidents is to make them social errors. The automobile has created a new social order on the streets and highways, and we haven't yet had time to evolve social customs such as we have in other fields of human relations. The time is coming when traffic violations will be looked upon much as lying, rudeness, or dishonesty is now; and people will refrain because of social pressure.*"

Freedom of the American Road - 1956
Ford Motor Company

While this photo of a 1951 Oldsmobile 88 is too tight to see the front of the car, what does show is interesting for several reasons. The Olds was rear-ended on an Ohio street in 1957. The car was badly rusted as evidenced by the fender area around the rear wheel. The force of the impact, assuming the floorboards were also rusty, caused the front seat to break loose and tip over. After the accident, the rear door was pried almost off its hinges, presumably to allow the safe removal of the driver and passengers, if injured. And yes, that's the corner of the gas tank jutting out from under the bumper. Note the 1956 Oldsmobile parked across the street. (Lloyd A. Himes photo)

This 1952 Nash Rambler Custom was involved in a fender bender in New York in 1958. The front of an early Volkswagen Beetle is visible in the background. (Ronald Marzlock photo)

Someone with the initials H.H. was the owner of this 1952 Mercury Monterey damaged in a 1960 accident in New York. H.H., along with his (her?) initials, accessorized the Mercury with a spotlight, fender-mounted rear view mirrors, steering wheel wrap, running lights and whip antenna. (Ronald Marzlock photo)

Based on the worn appearance of the front chrome trim, this 1952 Cadillac convertible was a road veteran prior to being involved in a sideswipe accident in New York in the early 1960s. Note the 1953 Cadillac wire wheels installed on the car. (Ronald Marzlock photo)

Kenneth H. Ahrens of Dover, Ark., writes: "This is the 1953 Henry J that I wrecked in 1957. It was my uncle's car and I was 16 and had just gotten my driver's license, although I had been driving since age 11: Kaisers, Frazers, Jeeps and even some early-1940s International dump trucks. I fell asleep and left the pavement, glanced off a rock wall (entrance to a roadside park) and then hit the second rock wall head-on. It was ass over elbows from there. Fortunately, I was not injured but my uncle was not happy with me." (Kenneth H. Ahrens photos)

New York's Henry Hudson Parkway in late-1957 was the scene of a multi-car pileup that included a 1953 Chevrolet Bel Air that jumped a highway divider strip and landed on top of the 1952 Ford. Firemen were called to the scene to hose down the fuel that leaked from one of the cars involved in the crash. (Peter Kanze photo)

A 1951 Buick was rear-ended by a 1953 DeSoto with the cars then ending up on opposite sides of the road. The accident occurred in the mid-1950s on a rural stretch of road, but that didn't deter a crowd from gathering. (Tim Bennett photos)

An interesting fact about speed and safety has just been turned up in special studies made by the National Safety Council. This research shows that the speeding driver who figured in an accident was generally helped to have the accident by contributory negligence on the part of the other fellow. The same study disclosed that this was not nearly so often true in the case of drunken drivers. A large percentage of them seemed able to have accidents without any help! In fact, the other fellow might be utterly blameless, and still be hit.

Seven Roads to Safety - 1939

Paul G. Hoffman (president of Studebaker)

How the 1953 Chevrolet came to rest on top of the Corvette is a mystery due to the fact that the top Chevy's passenger side is also caved in suggesting a collision with another vehicle or object before the secondary impact with the Vette. Law enforcement personnel on the scene inspected the wreckage with what would appear to be little hope for survivors in the Corvette. The crash happened in New York in 1956. (Stephen R. Behling photo)

Joseph DeSantis of Lynn, Mass., writes: "This was my 1953 Oldsmobile 88. While I was in the army serving overseas in the late-1950s, my brother hot-wired the car and was drag racing on Highland Avenue in Salem, Mass. He lost control of the Olds and rolled it down an embankment. He was not injured until I got home!" A Chevrolet tow truck and towing dolly under the rear wheels were used to move the car from the accident scene. (Joseph DeSantis photo)

A pair of Buick Specials, a 1953 (left) and 1954, collided at an intersection in Elwood, Ind., in the early-1960s with the 1954 Buick ending up wrapped around a power pole. The Indiana license plate on the front Buick reads "Safety Pays." (Larry Burwell photo)

It doesn't appear as if there's anything salvageable from this 1953 Chevrolet Bel Air convertible that got twisted and crushed in a 1958 accident in Ohio. (Robert Gilder photo)

No car could be a match for a tree the size of the one this 1953 Mercury slammed into in Holliston, Mass. Note the "flipper" hubcap on the front wheel. (Charlie Harper photo)

A real challenge for the tow truck operator was how to retrieve this 1953 Willys from a drainage ditch in Holliston, Mass. The car appears not to have suffered too much damage on the trip into the ditch, and the driver was probably more em-barrassed than injured. (Charlie Harper photo)

This primered and body filler-laden 1953 Ford was in rough shape before it crashed and flipped over in Maryland in 1963. None of the four tires match, and the driver's side rear is worn down to the cords. The car had some mild custom touches such as the flush taillights. The police officer behind the car is directing traffic around the shattered glass littering the highway. (Lawrence J. Gaddis/Martin L. Best photo)

Reminiscent of a carnival ride on the bumper cars, this chain reaction collision on Wickham Avenue in Middletown, N.Y., involved (l-to-r) a Hudson Hornet, 1940 Chevrolet and a 1954 Pontiac. It would appear that all the drivers of the cars involved are gathered behind the Pontiac trying to sort out what happened. Note all the interesting petroliana in the Esso service station window. (Marvin H. Cohen photo)

Fog and rain on the New Jersey Turnpike in late-1959 caused a nine-car pileup. One of the cars involved was this 1954 Buick. Police officers used flares and hand signals to direct traffic around the disabled car. (Peter Kanze photo)

What appears to be a roadside fence pole and cable is visible under this 1954 Hudson Hornet involved in a collision in New York in 1960. Note that even the passenger side door handle got sheared off in the accident. (Ronald Marzlock photo)

A 1960 Ford police car was dispatched to the scene of an accident involving a 1954 Chevrolet Bel Air convertible. The crash occurred in New York in 1960. (Ronald Marzlock photo)

This 1954 Chevrolet pickup operated by a Silver Spring, Md., brick contractor rolled over several times in 1958 and ended up in a field near a snow fence. The gouges in the turf are where the truck dug in during its gyrations. The contents of the bed landed in a heap away from the truck. (Lawrence J. Gaddis/Martin L. Best photo)

From the showroom floor to the body shop would seem to be the route taken by this 1954 Ford Crestline Victoria wrecked in a collision with another vehicle on a New York street. A Chevrolet tow truck is visible behind the Ford. (Ronald Marzlock photo)

Jim Balfour of Walpole, Mass., writes: "This photo was taken on a Friday evening in August of 1959 at the intersection of Route One and Dean Street in Norwood, Mass. This was and is a busy and dangerous road, although it has been improved considerably. The fire lieutenant in the center of the photo recalled that all the people involved in the crash survived, but they were a little banged up. The wrecker was from Ed's Auto Body and it's a Dodge from the 1940s." The cars involved in the pileup (l-to-r) were a 1955 Plymouth station wagon, 1955 Chrysler and 1956 Ford station wagon. (Jim Balfour photo)

A high-speed sudden stop can be no more graphically represented than with this 1954 Mercury Monterey that sailed off the Henry Hudson Parkway offramp in New York and into the side of a building in 1962. The Mercury was occupied by three teenagers, who were being chased by police. The youths' joyride was also their last ride. (Peter Kanze photo)

A tow truck operator searched for a place to attach tow hooks to remove this 1954 Mercury involved in a head-on collision on New York's Cross County Parkway in 1958. The firetrucks in the background were dispatched to the accident scene to put out the fire that erupted in the station wagon that the Mercury collided with. (Peter Kanze photo)

Aside from the errant seat cushion and missing rear window, from the driver's side (above) this 1954 Mercury Monterey looked fine. The view from the opposite side (below) told a different story; one involving the car grinding against a tree on a residential street in New York in 1955. The Merc was mildly customized with two-tone paint and dual exhaust. Note the Chevrolet pickup with tow boom used to remove the car from the accident scene. (Ronald Marzlock photos)

A 1955 Pontiac (background) and 1953 Oldsmobile were involved in this head-on collision in Maryland in 1958. Tire marks on the wet pavement showed the paths of travel of each car, which both came to rest on the wrong sides of the road. (Lawrence J. Gaddis/Martin L. Best photo)

This head-on crash on a residential Maryland street in 1959 involved a 1955 Mercury station wagon, which came to rest in someone's yard, and a 1948 Chevrolet. That's the Chevy's front bumper on the ground between the wrecked cars. (Lawrence J. Gaddis/Martin L. Best photo)

Had this 1955 Buick not been stopped by the tree, several cars and a gravel truck parked in the background were next in its path. The Buick left a Maryland highway in 1958 and jumped a ditch prior to hitting the tree. Damage to the rear fender and bumper suggest the car was hit on the highway, which caused its driver to lose control. (Lawrence J. Gaddis/Martin L. Best photo)

A two car crash in 1958 at an intersection in Washington, D.C., involved a 1956 Oldsmobile (left) and a 1953 Chevrolet. The man with the toolbox appears to be a fire department official who was sent to the accident scene as a precautionary measure. Note the police motorcycle parked behind the power pole in the background. (Lawrence J. Gaddis/Martin L. Best photo)

Beyond the obvious "horseshoed" front end, the best indicator of how hard this 1955 Oldsmobile 88 impacted the tree was the bent steering wheel caused by the driver bracing for the crash. Barely visible in the background is the grille and headlights of a 1961 Ford police car. (Ronald Marzlock photo)

A tow truck from the Esso service station in Holliston, Mass., hauled in a 1955 Oldsmobile 88 Holiday sedan that appears to have been hit by a train in 1956. The entire driver's side of the car was ripped open and the Olds was twisted from the impact. (Charlie Harper photo)

Two views of a 1955 Chevrolet Bel Air that slammed into a tree in Holliston, Mass., in 1960. Note the fender markers attached to the Chevy's headlight rims. (Charlie Harper photos)

All accidents are terrible but what could be worse than crashing into an officer of the law, which is exactly what happened in this wreck at the intersection of Scottsville Road and Ballantyne Road in New York in 1957. A 1955 Chevrolet 150 Handyman station wagon partially drove over a sheriff's Harley-Davidson Duo-Glide, causing the motorcycle to leak oil all over the road. The accident report must have been interesting reading! (Stephen R. Behling photo)

Towed to a service station side lot after the accident, this 1955 Chevrolet Bel Air was destroyed in a head-on collision. Note the angle of the steering wheel. (Ronald Marzlock photo)

At first glance it's a mystery how this 1955 Chevrolet Bel Air could have slid into the power pole unless it was being driven on the sidewalk! But two clues reveal what really happened. The tire mark on the curb and the scratch marks on the street side of the pole suggest the car skidded backwards off the street and impacted the pole and then spun clockwise around the pole. The crash occurred in Maryland in 1958. (Lawrence J. Gaddis/Martin L. Best photo)

Maybe it was the great sale on "Outdoor Living Specials" that caused the driver of this 1955 Ford Fairlane Sunliner to crash through the front window of a store on North Street in Middletown, N.Y. The tow truck extracting the Ford from the building drew quite a crowd. (Marvin H. Cohen photo)

This 1955 Ford Fairlane Victoria was mangled in a head-on crash in Ohio in 1959. (Lloyd A. Himes photo)

A 1955 Ford Customline caked with mud was attended to after a roll-over accident on a dirt road in Maryland in 1958. An American-LaFrance firetruck was dispatched to the accident scene. (Lawrence J. Gaddis/Martin L. Best photo)

A diversion for the patrons at the bar in the background, this 1955 Ford Country Squire station wagon was involved in a two car crash on Hawkins Avenue in New York. Note the ice shed to the right of the bar. (Ronald Marzlock photo)

In 1957, a New York sanitation truck was used to hoist a 1956 Chrysler out of the East River after the car had plunged off the pier the day before. It doesn't appear that there was much concern about causing further damage to the car while getting it back on the pier on its wheels. (Peter Kanze photo)

A pair of Oldsmobile 88s, a 1956 (left) and 1951, collided head-on on Cross Bay Boulevard in New York in 1957 in what would appear to be a fatal accident. Amazingly, all occupants of both cars lived to drive another day. Note the well-equipped police truck in the background. (Peter Kanze photo)

The hood of this 1955 Dodge was torn off the car as it barrel-rolled into a roadside stretch of woods. Note that the rear seat back was dislodged in the crash exposing the spare tire in the trunk. (Peter Kanze photo)

The aftermath of this Ohio accident can only be termed bizarre! The 1956 Ford Fairlane Sunliner rolled over and landed between a pair of residential front step railings with the top of the car not touching the ground. From this angle, the Ford appears relatively undamaged except for its windshield. (Lloyd A. Himes photo)

Locomotive 6192 literally impaled this 1956 Ford Fairlane Fordor that tried to beat the train at a crossing and lost. Note how the roof sheet metal separated from the support pillars. (Jack Sevier photo)

Not the first model that comes to mind when speaking of Checker taxis, but this 1956 Checker was a New York taxi and was involved in a collision in 1958. Upon close examination, for only a two-year old car, this Checker saw hard duty and all the dings and chipped paint suggest the car was involved in several scrapes prior to this fender bender. (Ronald Marzlock photo)

> *Since most motor cars of the early 1900s could not travel faster than 15 miles an hour, it would seem — contrasting this with the speeds of today — that serious accidents could not then have occurred. But photographs from half-a-century past reveal mangled and twisted wrecks which appear very similar to those which happen on present-day highways.*
>
> *The automobile, of itself — as many people have pointed out — has never injured anybody. It is the careless, thoughtless, incompetent, inebriated, or sleepy driver who creates the havoc, endangering his own life, the lives of those who ride with him, and the safety of other motorists, as well as pedestrians.*
>
> **Wheels Across America** - 1959
> Clarence P. Hornung

Two views of a 1956 Ford Victoria with Florida license plates, which had its top smashed flat (below) and passenger side peeled open in a 1960 crash in Maryland. Why the driver's door vent window was spared from the flattening is a mystery. The totality of damage to the car suggests it rolled over (several times?). (Lawrence J. Gaddis/Martin L. Best photos)

Not to be confused with an import model Ford, the photo was printed reversed. In either direction, though, the car was wrecked. This 1956 Mainline Fordor slid into a power pole in Maryland in 1958. (Lawrence J. Gaddis/Martin L. Best photo)

If not for the taillight and remaining half piece of rear fender script it would be difficult to identify this twisted hulk as a 1956 Ford Thunderbird. The convertible was rammed broadside at high speed on U.S. 31 in Indianapolis in 1957 (Peter Kanze photo)

A new fender, headlight and a bath and this 1956 Ford Thunderbird would have looked like a showroom model. Note that the bird emblem was missing from this T-bird's nose, and it doesn't appear as though it was knocked off in the accident. (Ronald Marzlock photo)

Even with all the devastation this accident caused, the first thing noticed is the 1956 Ford Thunderbird's custom paint scheme. The crash, which happened in Ohio in 1957, knocked down power lines. One line fell into the engine compartment of the car. A gloved hand visible above the raised hood removed a cut line from over the Ford. Note the upright angle of the T-bird's steering wheel. An electric company utility truck (background) was dispatched to the accident scene. (Stephen R. Behling photo)

A 1956 Lincoln had a run-in with a 1959 Pontiac Bonneville Vista (background) in New York in 1960. The Lincoln was definitely a candidate for a body shop repair project. (Ronald Marzlock photo)

Slick road conditions likely played a part in this accident. A 1956 Pontiac skidded off the street and into a tree, almost dead center. If the gentleman behind the wheel was the driver, he seemed quite bored with the whole incident! (Ronald Marzlock photo)

A 1956 Lincoln plowed into the back of a rusty, derelict-laden transport trailer parked on a New York street in 1960. Ironically, after the crash the Lincoln's undamaged headlight illuminated the massive trailer, which for unknown reasons was not originally seen in time to avoid hitting. Up close (below), the destruction of the Lincoln is evident. The hulks on the trailer (above) were a 1953 Packard, 1951 Dodge convertible, 1952 Buick Super, 1951 Chevrolet and 1951 Chrysler Windsor. (Ronald Marzlock photos)

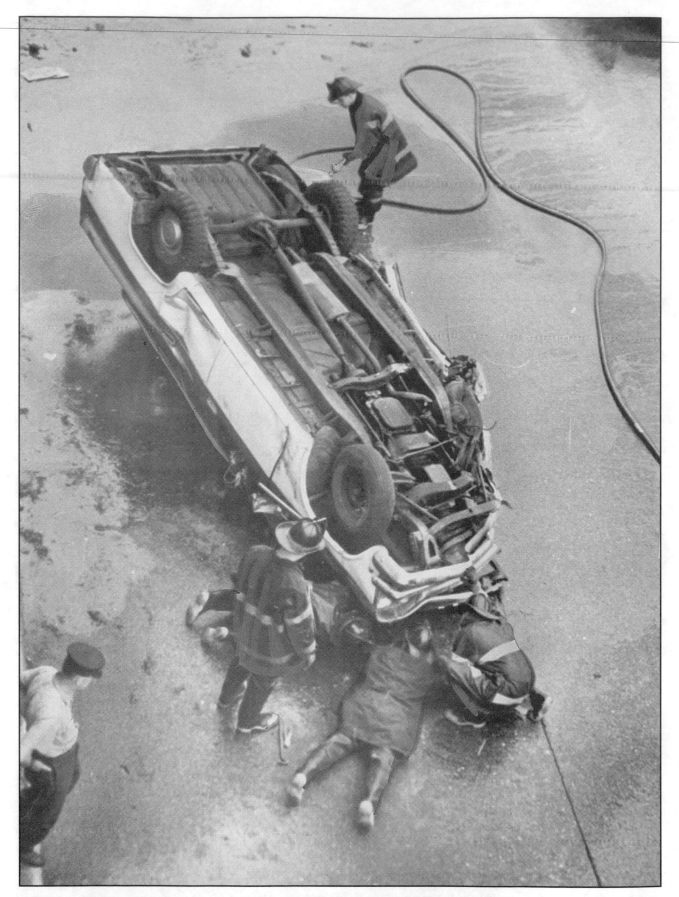

A group of firemen attempted to extricate the driver of this overturned 1957 Dodge station wagon, which crashed into a light standard and rolled over on the West Side Highway in New Jersey in 1962. The firemen were called to the accident scene to hose down the gasoline that leaked from the Dodge. (Peter Kanze photo)

After colliding with another vehicle not shown, this 1957 Dodge Custom Royal Lancer convertible came to rest on a sidewalk and bumped up against a mailbox. The accident happened in New York in 1958. Note the "square-Bird" behind the stop sign in the background. (Ronald Marzlock photo)

Virginia Koehler of Abington, Pa., writes: "This 1957 Imperial belonged to my grandfather. His daughter took the car to a family party in 1961 and the battery went dead. Four uncles offered to get it started for her when it was time for her to leave. One uncle drove, since he had a similar car and 'knew everything,' while the other three uncles pushed the car down a hill. The lights weren't used and the only person who didn't know the street was a dead end was the uncle driving. Needless to say, as soon as the car started the uncle driving revved the engine and the car smashed into the tree at the end of the street. Since everyone had enjoyed the party beverages so much, they all started laughing. No one was injured, and there were many versions as to how the Imperial ended up 'hugging' the tree. The next morning my grandfather drove the car home and waited for the towing service to pick it up." (Virginia Koehler photo)

Just visible in the background is the 1954 Chevrolet that this 1957 Plymouth collided with in New York in 1960. Note how worn the Plymouth's front tire's inner surface was suggesting alignment problems prior to the crash. (Ronald Marzlock photo)

The 1949 Plymouth in the foreground was only one-half of this 1958 accident. The 1957 Chrysler (in the background with its lights on) was the car that the Plymouth rammed into at a Maryland intersection. Police attended to the passenger in the Chrysler while a firetruck arrived on the scene to hose down the gasoline spilled from the Chrysler. Note the trail of spilled gas leading back to the Chrysler from where the officer stood in the intersection. (Lawrence J. Gaddis/ Martin L. Best photo)

Every Chevrolet enthusiast's worst nightmare! This all-1957 Chevy crash occurred in Maryland in November 1957 when the cars were near new. The police car was a 210 model as was the Chevy in the ditch. The Chevy with the battered front end was a Bel Air. The car in the background was a 1957 Buick. (Lawrence J. Gaddis/Martin L. Best photo)

Little remained of the front end of this 1957 Chevrolet Bel Air station wagon after it collided with a truck in Genoa, Ohio, in 1963. After the crash, a fire erupted in the Chevy's engine compartment, being inspected by the onlookers at the accident scene. Note that the frame of the car was almost touching the ground behind the front wheel. (Peter Kanze photo)

Looking as if it was used in a car bombing, this 1957 Chevrolet struck one of those concrete pillars in the background at a high rate of speed. The crash occurred in New York in 1959. Amazingly, while the three passengers in the car weren't so fortunate, the driver walked away from this mess with nothing more than a bruised knee! Note the section of driveshaft next to the front wheel. (Peter Kanze photo)

A 1958 Ford police car was parked on the side of the road while its officers investigated inside the barn where a car flew off the road and crashed through the wall. The accident happened in New Jersey in 1959 and alcohol and excessive speed were involved. A 1953 Buick passed behind the onlookers gathered on the hill. Note what appears to be a fender from the "barned" car on the roof. (Peter Kanze photo)

The worst view of this 1958 crash is the other side of the car. This 1957 Ford Country Sedan was involved in a head-on collision with another vehicle and got shoved into the railing of a narrow Maryland bridge. Note that the first impact was so severe that it tore the driver's side wheel off and it ended up under the frame holding the car up off the bridge. The open tailgate suggests that's how the injured were removed from the Ford. (Lawrence J. Gaddis/Martin L. Best photo)

A car not often seen today, this 1957 Ford Fairlane 500 Club Sedan ran off the road near Elwood, Ind., and rolled over into a rain-soaked farm field. (Larry Burwell photo)

This 1957 Ford Fairlane 500 Club Sedan was involved in a crash on a residential New York street, which resulted in its front-hinged hood popping up from the impact. The tow truck was already at the accident scene to remove the Ford from the street. (Ronald Marzlock photo)

A police officer used the trunklid of this mildly customized 1957 Ford Fairlane 500 to write up the report on the accident involving the Ford. The fender bender occurred in New York in 1960. The Ford's custom treatment included Edsel hubcaps, dual outside rear view mirrors, headlight "eyelids" and removal of hood ornament and Fairlane script from the front of the car.

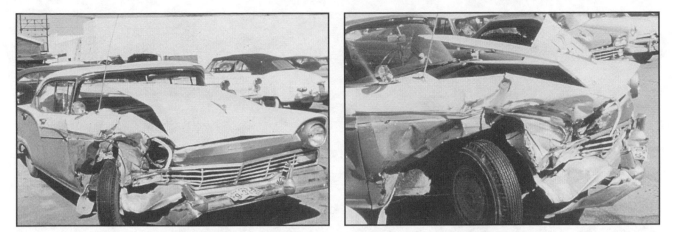

Wayne "Bud" Mikkelson of Milbank, S.D., writes: "I purchased this 1957 Ford Fairlane 500 Town Victoria new in 1957. My father-in-law borrowed the car to go to California in the spring of 1958. While in Los Angeles, he made a left-hand turn into two lanes of oncoming traffic. A car coming from the other direction hit him in the right front. My father-in-law wasn't hurt, but his wife suffered a concussion and four broken ribs. They had the Ford repaired in California and drove it back to South Dakota." (Wayne Mikkelson photos)

A Maryland police officer directed traffic around a 1958 Ford Fairlane that appears to have been involved in a two vehicle crash, the other car or truck not shown. The impact caused the Ford's front-hinged hood to spring open. A 1958 Plymouth was driving by in the other lane. The accident occurred Christmas day in 1958. (Lawrence J. Gaddis/Martin L. Best photo)

Mixin' booze with gasolene
creates power that can't be
controlled. Power out of control
is a destroyin' man-killin' beast.

Stay Alive - 1928
Marcus Dow speaking as Jim the Truckman

Based on the pieces of gravel and the rock in its grille area, this 1958 Chrysler Saratoga must have rear-ended a gravel hauler truck or a trailer filled with gravel. The accident happened in New York in 1960. In the background were a pair of Fords. (Ronald Marzlock photo)

This gentleman obviously had the "Mercury blues" after being involved in an accident in New York in 1960. The 1958 Mercury Monterey appears to have rear-ended another vehicle not shown. A 1959 Ford police car was parked behind the Mercury. (Ronald Marzlock photo)

A slippery brick street probably was a factor in this two vehicle crash in Ohio. While only this 1958 Buick is shown, the amount of damage to it would suggest a tow truck (behind Buick) was also needed for the other vehicle involved. Note that the Buick was pointed in the wrong direction on a one-way street based on the cars parked in the background. (Lloyd A. Himes photo)

It's almost as if a bite was taken out of the side of this 1958 Buick Super. The well-kept car was involved in a crash in New York in 1960. (Ronald Marzlock photo)

A 1958 Buick Special with its "toothless grin" look after a collision in New York in 1960. Just visible is the siren of a Chevrolet police car that was parked behind the Buick. (Ronald Marzlock photo)

Fiberglass does not bend, it breaks, as was evidenced by the damage to this 1958 Corvette involved in a head-on collision in New York in 1960. A 1956 Chevy convertible and 1959 Chevy police car were in the background. No doubt, this beauty was repaired and provided many more miles and smiles. (Ronald Marzlock photo)

A 1954 Chevrolet (left) and a new 1958 Chevy Bel Air collided head-on in Maryland in 1958. The Bel Air's bent steering wheel is evidence of how hard the impact was. (Lawrence J. Gaddis/Martin L. Best photo)

Alan Roth of Lakewood, Ohio, writes: "This 1958 Chevy Biscayne was my first car. I was 18 and had it six weeks. On a Friday night in May of 1967, I was traveling too fast to negotiate a left-hand turn. The car rolled over and hit three trees. I was charged $90 for loss of life expectancy on the trees. Fortunately, I was uninjured." (Alan Roth photos)

> *Little safety rules is bigger*
> *than the car you drive.*
> *Without 'em your car would*
> *soon be just a pile of junk.*
> **Stay Alive** - 1928
> Marcus Dow speaking as Jim the Truckman

Larry Burwell of Frankton, Ind., was a newspaper photographer from 1957 to 1963. He photographed this 1958 Chevrolet Impala convertible, which was involved in an accident in Elwood, Ind. He writes: "The Impala knocked down a large overhead railroad crossing signal, two cast iron street light posts and six parking meters. Four minors fled the scene with minor injuries." (Larry Burwell photo)

For many years the injuries and fatalities resulting from the use of the automobile were accepted rather fatalistically. They were regarded, almost generally, as the logical and inevitable price society must pay for its newest and greatest form of individual rapid transportation.
Seven Roads to Safety - 1939
Paul G. Hoffman (president of Studebaker)
(quoted from the book's foreword by
John W. Darr, director of CIT Safety Foundation)

146

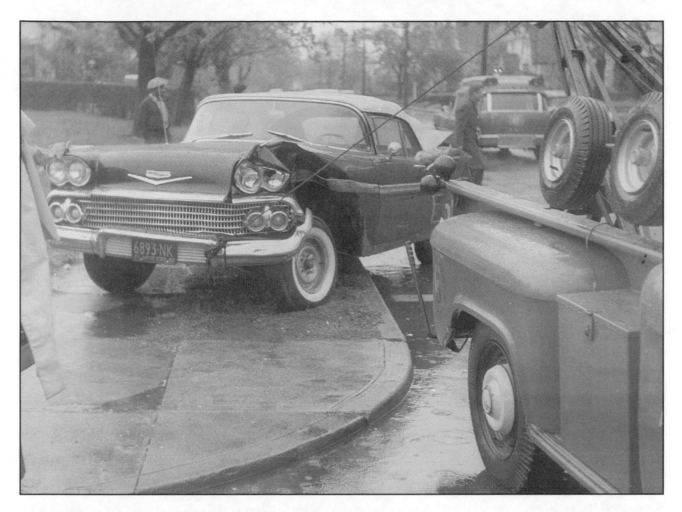

A Cadillac ambulance (above) pulled away in the background with siren lit, so the driver of this 1958 Chevrolet Impala convertible or the other vehicle (not shown) it collided with must have received injuries. A cable from the tow truck was attached to the Chevy's bumper to pull the car off the sidewalk. The crash happened in New York in 1960. (Ronald Marzlock photos)

Based on the blistered paint on the fender it appears that an engine compartment fire flared up in this 1959 Dodge Coronet convertible after it was involved in a collision in New York in 1960. (Ronald Marzlock photo)

A 1959 Dodge Coronet came to rest over a sewer grate after being involved in a two car crash at a Maryland intersection. Note the police officers in the background who were investigating the accident scene, one talking to a young boy who probably witnessed the crash. (Lawrence J. Gaddis/Martin L. Best photo)

A New York sanitation truck was used to hoist this 1959 Ford Fairlane 500 out of the East River after it plunged into the water in 1961. The car had crashed through steel railing on the pier before sailing into the water. (Peter Kanze photo)

A 1959 Ford embedded itself in the rear of a 1953 Plymouth in this two car crash in New York. A police officer at the scene inspected the Ford's engine compartment after the impact sprung the reverse-hinged hood. Note that a piece of debris from the crash got wedged under the Plymouth's rear tire. (Ronald Marzlock photo)

Middle Island Road in New York in 1961 was the scene of a head-on collision involving a 1957 Chevrolet (left) and a 1960 Oldsmobile. Note the flatness of each car's front end suggesting one of the cars was in the wrong lane and the collision was direct bumper-to-bumper. A 1960 Plymouth police car was parked in the background. (Peter Kanze photo)

Broken fiberglass and twisted chrome were a result of a two car crash in New York involving this 1959 Corvette. The Vette rear-ended another vehicle, not shown, causing gasoline to be leaked and necessitating having firemen at the accident scene. (Ronald Marzlock photo)

The railroad crossing signal in the background would at first suggest that this 1959 Pontiac Bonneville Vista Sedan was clipped in the rear by the train, but more likely the damage was done by another vehicle and the crash scene just happened to be at a railroad crossing. The crash occurred in New York in 1961. Quite a group of onlookers gathered to get a better look. (Ronald Marzlock photo)

Route 93 in Tewksbury, Mass., in 1962 was the scene of a 22 car pileup that included a late-1950s Mack truck. Just about every automaker was represented in this crash, and fortunately there were no fatalities. Fog was listed as the cause of the pileup. Note the Dodge Power Wagon tow truck in the background. (Peter Kanze photo)

The owner of this new 1959 Chevrolet Impala convertible with the potent 348 cubic inch V-8 didn't have much time to enjoy his ragtop before it was damaged in a crash. The accident occurred near Elwood, Ind., in 1960. No doubt, after a stint in the body shop this Chevy was back on the road. (Larry Burwell photo)

Two views of a 1959 Pontiac Bonneville that crashed in New York in 1960. The smudges on the damaged area of the Pontiac suggest this was a one car accident, and the Pontiac hit a dirt embankment or tree surrounded by dirty snow. Note the sheared off door handle. The Chevrolet tow truck operators (below) lifted the Pontiac off the guardrail prior to removing it from the accident scene. (Ronald Marzlock photos)

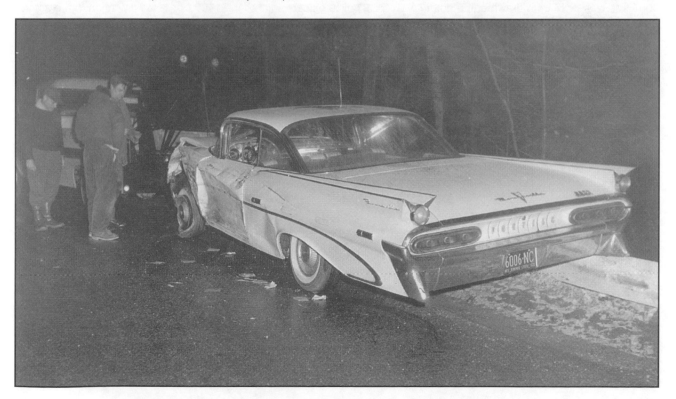

Complete with flight path drawn out, a pair of New York police officers point to the 1960 Ford station wagon that crashed through an iron railing and plunged onto the Henry Hudson Parkway in 1962. Note the Ford's tailgate, which broke off on impact, in the back of the car. A 1961 Plymouth police car was parked in front of the Ford. Other traffic at the time included a Chrysler and a Pontiac and Cadillac in the opposite lane. (Peter Kanze photo)

A pool of radiator fluid formed under this battered 1960 Metropolitan convertible involved in a collision in New York in 1960. The Metro's front bumper was full of paint from whatever it collided with. (Ronald Marzlock photo)

This 1960 Chevrolet Impala Sport Sedan was actually involved in two crashes near Elwood, Ind. The car was hit broadside and then left the road and slammed head-on into a tree. Barely visible in the background parked in front of the "Drive Inn" was a 1960 Studebaker Lark Marshal police car. A 1959 Chevy Impala with custom wheel covers passed behind the Sport Sedan, which itself featured aftermarket clear plastic seat covers. (Larry Burwell photo)

Another few feet and this 1960 Chevrolet would have dropped into Lake Michigan. The car skidded upside down on icy ground for 100 yards after it left Outer Beach Drive in Chicago in 1960. The driver walked away from this crash with only cuts and bruises. (Peter Kanze photo)

The downed power lines that surrounded this 1960 Pontiac suggest the driver and passenger were "trapped" in the car until power could be cut off. The Pontiac left Highway 25 in New York and smashed into a power pole, cracking it at its base. (Ronald Marzlock photo)

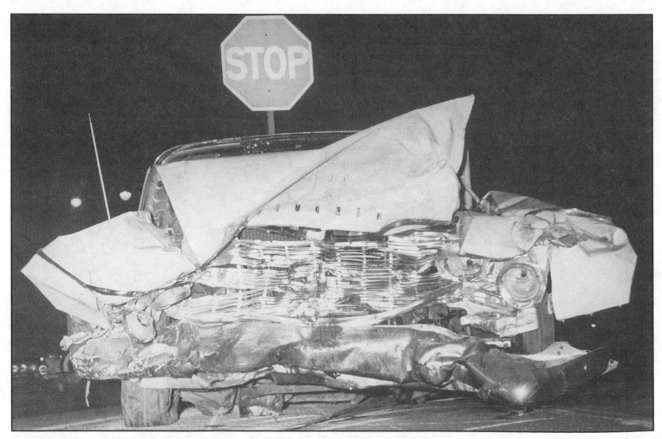

This 1960 Plymouth stopped all right, but not in the manner intended by the road sign looming behind the car. The Plymouth was involved in a two car crash in New York in 1963. (Peter Kanze photo)

A rain-slick highway was the cause of this accident involving a bus (not shown), the Chevrolet in the background and the 1960 Chrysler in front. The bus slid out of control and crossed the centerline, colliding with these two oncoming cars. A tow truck (with boom lights on) was parked in the background to begin cleanup of the accident scene. (Peter Kanze photo)

A sad ending for someone who gave much happiness to others, comedian Ernie Kovacs was killed when his 1961 Corvair station wagon skidded out of control on wet pavement and struck a utility pole driver's door first. The accident occurred in California in 1962. (Peter Kanze photo)

Route 20 in North Ridgeville, Ohio, in 1962 was the scene of this head-on collision involving a 1960 Pontiac Bonneville (background) and a 1960 Mercury. The towing chains were already attached to the Mercury for the car to be removed from the highway. Note the Mercury's sun visors sticking out from the impact. (Robert Gilder photo)

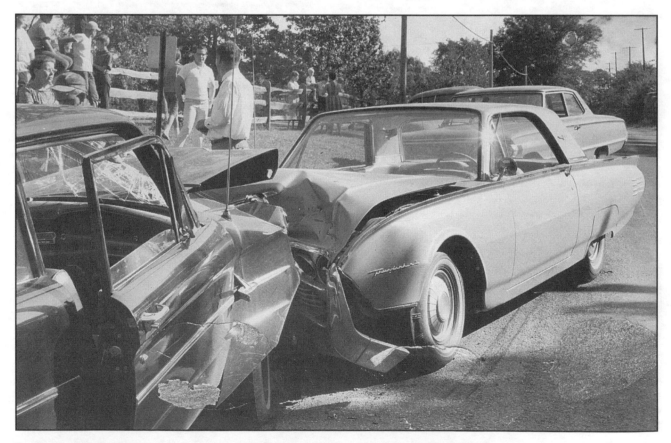

A pair of Fords collided head-on in while traveling on Case Road in North Ridgeville, Ohio, in the mid-1960s. One of the cars in the crash was a 1961 Thunderbird, which, from a damage standpoint, appears to have held up well compared to the other car involved in the accident. (Robert Gilder photo)

Two views of a new 1961 Mercury Monterey convertible that was literally torn in two after impacting a tree in New York in late 1960. A large portion of the car including the rear end assembly was launched on impact out of camera range. Note the 1960 Plymouth police car in the background. The damage to the front corner (above) of the Mercury was caused by impact with something prior to the impact with the tree. (Ronald Marzlock photos)

A rusty 1961 Chrysler and a late-1960s Chevrolet Impala were involved in this head-on collision on Cambridge Street in Allston, Mass. Several firemen were called to the scene to lend assistance. A 1966 Chevy police car was parked at the intersecting street in the background and its officer was directing traffic away from the accident scene. (John Greenland photo)

Hard to believe, but the two youths walked away from this destroyed 1962 Chevrolet that was shredded in a collision with a tree in 1964. The gentleman surveying the wreckage drove to the scene in the Mercury parked at the service station in the background. The car's six-cylinder engine was visible with the hood popped open from the impact. (Peter Kanze photo)

Two views of a new 1961 Pontiac convertible that was hit broadside by another vehicle that was equipped with what appears was a protruding bumper. The accident occurred in a residential area of New York in late 1960. The car (below) was already "on the hook" for the tow to the dealership body shop. (Ronald Marzlock photos)

The title on this photo is "Time Expired," which is reflected in the window of the parking meter next to this 1963 Chevrolet that crashed into a light standard. The accident occurred on Brighton Avenue in Allston, Mass. Based on the angle of impact, the Chevy must have slid backwards or was hit on the passenger side and "shoved" into the pole. A VW Beetle, AMC, Chevy and Olds were parked in the background. (John Greenland photo)

A 1961 Chevrolet Bel Air (left) collided with a 1963 Corvette, which disintegrated upon impact, on a rain-slick road. Among the onlookers gathered behind the cars was a fireman whose duties probably included crowd control. (Jack Sevier photo)

A Harley-Davidson police motorcycle and 1963 Mercury Monterey were involved in this collision in Kansas City, Mo. A fire hose run from the firetruck in the background was set up to dilute the gas leaking from the obviously split tank on the Harley. Leaning in the driver's window, a fireman talked to the driver of the Mercury, who was presumably shaken from being involved in an accident and doubly so from colliding with an officer of the law. (William K. Miller photo)

Called a "flamboyant Ku Klux Klan attorney" by the media, Matt Murphy apparently fell asleep at the wheel of this 1964 Chrysler convertible and careened off an oncoming gasoline truck on Highway 11 in Tuscaloosa, Ala., in 1965. Murphy was fatally injured in the crash. The car was towed to a salvage yard from the accident scene. (Peter Kanze photo)

A 1964 Pontiac Tempest LeMans convertible hung precariously from this partially opened drawbridge in Miami, Fla., in 1966. Initially, the car was wedged windshield deep between the steel grate bridge surface and the concrete wall in front of the Pontiac's hood. After the three occupants of the car were safely removed, the car was secured to the grating and the drawbridge opened a bit. A tow truck operator (under rear bumper) then secured cables to the car so it could be moved back up the bridge. The drawbridge was then closed and the car was towed off. (Peter Kanze photo)

This 1964 Buick LeSabre was bent almost into an L-shape after impacting a tree. Note the broken, tilted power pole behind the car's hood, suggesting the Buick might have hit it first and then was stopped by the tree. A tow truck (background) was at the scene, but a flatbed might have been needed to haul this mess away. (Jack Sevier photo)

A Dodge Indiana State Police car was dispatched to the scene of a head-on crash involving a 1965 Buick and a 1953 Plymouth. Note the "Pass With Care" sign on the side of the road. (Jack Sevier photo)

This photo is titled "Making A New Exit" off Lincoln Street in Allston, Mass. A 1965 Plymouth got hit broadside and knocked through a chain-link fence into a rail yard. The cardboard box under the car appears to be litter and not related to the accident. (John Greenland photo)

The driver of this 1965 Chevrolet convertible, who was not wearing a seatbelt at the time of this crash, was ejected from the Chevy as it turned over on Route 76 in Ohio. The driver basically dusted himself off and escaped with only minor injuries. The tow truck operators hooked cables to the car's frame to right it before towing it away. (Robert Gilder photo)

A motorcycle collided with a 1965 Ford on a rain-slick street with devastating results for the cyclist. The handlebars of the motorcycle were bent back completely into a U-shape from the force of the impact. (Jack Sevier photo)

This 1967 Ford Falcon was photographed on the lot of an auto body in Allston, Mass., in 1971. The car hit either a pole or a tree, which left quite a dramatic indentation in the Ford. (John Greenland photo)

This 1966 Ford Mustang slid upside down down the concrete bridge foundation before crashing through the chain-link fence and coming to rest nose only on the ground. The Mustang originally slid out of control on the Verrazano-Narrows Bridge in New York in 1966 and was launched into the air after slamming into snow piled against the bridge railing. The car landed back end first on the sloped foundation and flipped onto its roof before sliding to a stop. (Peter Kanze photo)

A young man's pride and joy, a 1966 Ford Mustang, was wrecked in a 1971 collision in Massachusetts. (John Greenland photo)

This exotic all-aluminum bodied (coachwork by Gangloff) 1939 Bugatti cabriolet was wrecked in a 1968 three car crash in California. Owner Dr. Richard Riddell reports that he was traveling east approaching a westbound car stopped to turn. The driver of a car approaching the stopped westbound car was looking at the Bugatti and slammed into the stopped car, which in turn was shoved into the Bugatti. That collision caused the Bugatti to roll over. Dr. Riddell also reports that the Bugatti has since been rebuilt, including a new body. (Dr. Richard R. Riddell photo)

A 1957 Porsche Speedster convertible shows the result of rear-ending a much larger Pontiac in 1960. A police officer inspects the Porsche while two men, presumably the drivers of the two cars involved, appear to be discussing what happened. The tell-tale rain-slicked road may have been a factor in the accident. (Ronald Marzlock photo)

For reasons unknown, the driver of this BMW Isetta ran off a coastal California road and barrel rolled the minicar down onto the beach. (Isetta Johns photo)

Known as the "bug-eyed" Sprite, this late-1950s Austin-Healey appears sound at first glance but the sand on the headlights is evidence it was involved in a roll-over accident in 1960. A better indication is the windshield as well as the side mirrors being snapped off. No doubt this little beauty was repaired and gave its owner many more wind-in-the-hair miles of motoring pleasure. (Ronald Marzlock photo)

A soft-top roadster from the late-1950s or early-1960s, this Triumph TR-3A flattened a roadside signpost in an off-road collision. Note the headlight trim ring that ended up around the fender-mounted rear view mirror. This fun machine was a definite candidate for rebuilding. (Ronald Marzlock photo)

In 1972, this 1960s Porsche convertible was destroyed in a crash on Soldiers Field Road in Brighton, Mass. The sports car was towed to this field from the accident scene. (John Greenland photo)

This accident, which occurred at the intersection of Beacon Street and Claradon Street in Boston, Mass., involved a Volkswagen Type 3 Fastback (front) and a 1974 Toyota Corolla 1600. The felled light standard explains how the VW got bent, but how the Toyota ended up squashed from both sides is a mystery. Obviously, other vehicles not shown were also involved. (John Greenland photo)

For a time in September of 1941 West State Road in Alliance, Ohio, was known as the "Onion Highway" after this 1937 Ford truck flipped over tossing its load of vegetables onto the highway. The front tires on this Ford are worn out. Note the billboard for Fleet Wing Motor Oil in the background. (Frank A. Hoiles photo)

Truck #21 of the Inter-State System, a 1940 GMC, left the road west of Alliance, Ohio, in April of 1941 and jackknifed causing the frame of the tractor to kink and the roof of the sleeper cab to rip open. (Frank A. Hoiles photo)

A two vehicle crash at the intersection of State and Liberty Streets in Alliance, Ohio, in September of 1941 involved a late-1930s International tractor with trailer operated by Dearman Transport and a new 1941 Plymouth coupe. The truck rolled on top of the coupe and squashed a car that probably had extremely low mileage. The trailer was filled with wood and metal fencing. (Frank A. Hoiles photo)

A late-1930s International dump truck operated by Reber Fuel & Supply of Alliance, Ohio, lost control on a slippery street and left the road. The truck clipped a tree, which tore off the International's front wheel and fender, and came to rest in a ditch. An unidentified tow truck tried to pull the International back onto the street but only ended up doing a "wheelie" for lack of power. Men climbed aboard the front fenders of the wrecker for ballast, but even the extra weight didn't help! (Frank A. Hoiles photo)

Little careless actions
Of a million gents,
Makes a world of misery
From highway accidents.

Stay Alive - 1928
Marcus Dow speaking as Jim the Truckman

This International tractor pulling a Fruehauf flatbed trailer drove off the Ohio turnpike near Elyria in 1964 and burrowed into the ground. The sudden stop caused the coil of steel being hauled to break free and smash through the cab of the truck. The truck's driver was killed in this freak secondary collision. (Robert Gilder photo)

A roll-over accident and subsequent fire destroyed this mid-1950s White tractor, shown in a New York impound yard after being towed from the accident scene. (Peter Kanze photo)

What appears to be a Ford stepvan hauling Kistler's Quality Donuts hit a patch of ice on Route 10 in Ridgeville, Ohio, in 1964 and veered into a ditch and overturned. (Robert Gilder photo)

The 1955 Dodge Royal Lancer and its driver didn't stand a chance of surviving the head-on impact with the White tractor-trailer nor the secondary impact against the roadside tree. Contributing to this wreck on Route 10 in Ohio was the telltale snow that caused slippery road conditions. (Robert Gilder photo)

Freezing rain caused the driver of this 1961 Mercury Comet to lose control and slide into the path of this oncoming Kenworth tractor-trailer. The impact locked the vehicles' fronts together. The momentum of the Kenworth shoved the rear of the Mercury over the guardrail just enough to suspend it in midair. (Robert Gilder photo)

A tanker filled with 5,000 gallons of oil broke free from the tractor pulling it while traveling on Route 4 in New Jersey in 1961. The wayward tanker ended up rolling into a diner parking lot where it tipped over onto a 1961 Oldsmobile, crushing it and its unsuspecting driver. (Peter Kanze photo)

Ironically ending up against a tree with a "no truck or trailer parking" sign attached, a Chevrolet (left) tractor-trailer and International tractor-trailer carrying a load of hogs in its Fruehauf livestock trailer crashed head-on on Route 10 in Ohio. (Robert Gilder photo)

An attempt by this 1939 Dodge truck to beat the locomotive (background) at a crossing failed in this 1946 crash. The shredded Dodge was dragged after impact, scattering its parts along the way. (Peter Kanze photo)

This head-on collision on Route 10 in Ohio involved an International tractor with Thermo-King refrigeration trailer and a Fannie Farmer delivery truck. Note the snapped power pole draped over the trailer and hand-held fire extingulshers in the foreground. (Robert Gilder photo)

This Ford 950 tractor with Trailmobile trailer plowed into a 1964 Plymouth and 1956 Buick Special, causing the Buick to overturn. The force of the impact caused what was once a cab over engine tractor to become a cab beyond engine mess. (Jack Sevier photo)

A two-truck crash on Route 10 in Ridgeville, Ohio, involved a White tractor with Copco trailer hauling steel castings slamming into an unidentified jackknifed truck. (Robert Gilder photo)

No information was available for this accident so speculation is the truck's driver lost control of his tractor-trailer on icy roads. The vehicle just missed hitting a wooden road marker post, tore through strands of barbed wire and plunged down the embankment, which caused the trailer to break free of the tractor and tip over. When the truck stopped, other than needing a change of shorts the driver was okay and started to think about how to put a positive spin on what happened before informing the boss his load wouldn't reach its destination. The wrecker in the background is preparing to right the overturned trailer. (Greg Holmes photo)

An Ohio residential intersection in 1958 was the scene of this car-truck collision involving a late-1940s International truck and a 1955 Ford Ranch Wagon from Martin's Pastry Shop. The well-worn International appears undamaged, while the same cannot be said for the Ford or its load of pastries. (Lloyd Himes photo)

With the visible damage to the front of this mid-1930s International tractor it's apparent it hit something before overturning. The truck's trailer was an enclosed unit before coming apart in the roll-over. The crash occurred on State Highway 57 near Waldo, Wis. (Richard A. Williams photo)

A 1959 off-road excursion through the Maryland woods mangled the front end of this mid-1950s International dump truck. (Lawrence J. Gaddis/Martin L. Best photo)

The driver of this tractor-trailer rig heroically sacrificed his life in 1959 when the brakes on his truck failed and he purposely drove the vehicle into the entrance sidewall of the Lincoln Tunnel in New Jersey to keep from endangering other motorists. (Peter Kanze photo)

A 1956 International tractor received severe front end damage as a result of a collision with what appears to be a pole the way the bumper is caved in. A young man, probably not the truck's driver, surveys the damage. (Ronald Marzlock photo)

Two tractor-trailer rigs did a squeeze play on this 1961 Ford Thunderbird, which has suffered a ruptured fuel tank and has come to rest in a puddle of leaked gasoline. Note that the force of the impact has shoved the wheel and tire into the door cavity. (Jack Sevier photo)

A White tractor that couldn't stop in time rode up the back of a Ford Falcon, flattening its trunk area. Not even Samsonite luggage could have held up in that trunk. (Jack Sevier photo)

The 1952 Buick had its side peeled open by the empty 1961 GMC car transporter at an intersection near Elwood, Ind., in the early 1960s. Compared to the Buick, the GMC received only minor frontal damage. (Larry Burwell photo)

Workers attach tow hooks to this overturned 1940s Chevrolet delivery truck in preparation of putting it back on its wheels. The accident occurred in Middleton, N.Y., in 1948. Damage to the truck appears to be little more than cosmetic. Speculation on the cause of the wreck is that the vehicle was traveling too "swift." (Marvin H. Cohen photo)

As the cliché goes, not much stops mail delivery in the United States but whatever mail was being delivered by this Chevrolet got delayed after the step van slammed into a parked truck in a downtown setting. Obviously, traffic at the accident scene was stopped for the little girl to be standing where she is. (Ronald Marzlock photo)

This 1945 Brockway 260X tractor literally disintegrated in a 1950 roll-over accident in Middletown, N.Y. The rear axle assembly was torn from the chassis, as was the front wheel visible from this angle. (Marvin H. Cohen photo)

The driver of this 1950s Brockway tractor with trailer filled with cardboard lost control on a slushy Route 202 in Connecticut in 1958 and slid off the road and overturned. The truck was operated by the New Haven Board and Carton Company. (Peter Kanze photo)

Wolf's Motor Court near Elwood, Ind., was the scene of an early-1960s crash involving a 1962 Pontiac (below) and a late-1940s Ford tractor trailer (above) operated by Renner's Xpress. The Pontiac slammed into the rear of the Ford as it was turning into the motel, causing the truck to overturn. The Ford's underside is visible behind the Pontiac in the bottom photo. (Larry Burwell photos)

In what can only be described as choreographed jackknifing, a trio of late-1930s International tractors with trailers ended up off the road and stuck. It appears that the Advance Express trucks never touched! In the bottom photo, the cab was jackknifed so tightly against the trailer that the truck's driver had to exit through the passenger door. Obviously, the ice-covered roads had a part in this big rig ballet. (Greg Holmes photos)

Probably not quite what Chevrolet had in mind for a new car durability demonstration. A Chevrolet car transporter hauling a load of 1961 cars to the dealership had a Parkwood station wagon come loose and fall off. The Chevy must have hung up on its transmission or driveshaft, which saved the car from crashing to the pavement. Can you say demonstrator model! (Ronald Marzlock photo)

John Hislop Jr. writes: "In 1959, this load of new Volkswagens was en route to the VW dealer in Louisville, Ky., when the driver of the truck encountered a low bridge in Covington, Ky. Upon realizing his fate, he decided to speed up so as not to get 'stuck' and ended up making convertibles out of two sedans and a bus. That's my father (standing on top), John Hislop, the dealer, taking 'delivery' of the VWs. None of the Volkswagens on the lower level of the hauler sustained as much as a scratch!" (John Hislop Jr. photo)

The driver of this 1940s International cement mixer operated by Stewart Sand & Material Co. misjudged the clearance of the building opening and "brought down the house" on his truck. This accident occurred in Kansas City, Mo., in 1947. (William K. Miller photo)

A 1940s Chevrolet tractor with trailer operated by the Graves truck line plunged off a wooden bridge in Kansas City, Mo., in the mid-1940s and landed upside down in a lumber yard below. The cab remained relatively intact considering the drop. (William K. Miller photo)

The cab of this 1938 Chevrolet tractor was crushed from both ends after the truck first slammed head-on into a concrete safety island and then its trailer hauling livestock broke free and rolled forward into the driver's compartment. The crash occurred in Kansas City, Mo. Note the worn condition of the front tire. (William K. Miller photo)

The westbound lane of the Pennsylvania Turnpike near Carlisle was the scene of pile-up involving 14 tractor-trailer rigs as well as other vehicles in 1966. The blowing snow caused one truck to jackknife setting off a chain reaction of sliding and smashing big rigs. The Cadillac in the background appears to have stopped clear of the accident scene, but the car behind it must have took to the ditch to avoid the crash. (Peter Kanze photo)

City transit bus #16 operating in Jamaica, N.Y., collided with something blunt and tall as evidenced by the crease in the roof. It appears the bus is in the shop awaiting repair. (Ronald Marzlock photo)

A tow truck operator inspects the truck that slammed into the side of a Greyhound bus en route to San Antonio, Texas, in 1962. (Peter Kanze photo)

The driver of this intercity bus traveling from New York on Route 3 to New Jersey in 1963 lost control on a rain-slicked highway and crossed the center line before colliding with two oncoming vehicles. A police officer inspects the wreckage while a tow truck has lifted the bus in preparation for removing it from the accident scene. (Peter Kanze photo)

A GM bus loaded with servicemen en route to Fort Dix rammed the rear of a tractor trailer on the New Jersey turnpike in 1959. Both vehicles were traveling at highway speed when the collision occurred. (Peter Kanze photo)

This collision between a mid-1950s International school bus and a 1951 Chevrolet happened in Brooklyn, N.Y., in 1960. Fortunately, no one in either vehicle was injured. Both vehicles ended up on the sidewalk, with the only casualty in the accident being the fire hydrant knocked over by the bus. (Peter Kanze photo)

A blown tire caused the driver of this GMC 4000 school bus to lose control and smash into a fire hydrant followed by knocking over a telephone pole before coming to rest against a tree. Despite the severity of the impact with the three objects, only minor injuries were reported among the student passengers. (Peter Kanze photo)

AUTO RACING

The Lincoln ambulance parked and unattended in the background wasn't needed for the driver of this open wheel racer. The car flipped violently during a late 1920s race at Legion Ascot Speedway in California. (Bruce Craig Historic Racing Photos)

A group of men survey the damage to a crashed open wheel racer at Legion Ascot Speedway in California. The customized roadster pickup parked nearby was assigned to hauling track cleanup personnel. (Bruce Craig Historic Racing Photos)

A Packard tow vehicle is used to haul away the Gilmore Lion Head Special #2, which was severely bent in an October 29, 1933, roll-over crash at the five-eighths mile dirt oval Legion Ascot Speedway in California. Driver George Conners was slightly bruised in the wreck. (Bruce Craig Historic Racing Photos)

A modified late-1920s Lincoln tow vehicle from Haiden Auto Parts of Oakland, Calif., prepares to right a tipped and heavily damaged open wheel racer at Legion Ascot Speedway. The unpacked condition of Ascot's oiled dirt racing surface shows this wreck happened early in the program. (Bruce Craig Historic Racing Photos)

An added attraction after Rex Mays (#1, background) won the main event for open wheel cars was a roll-over exhibition by Prokop & Wards Hollywood Death Dodgers. The car is a 1936 Ford. Track location is not known. (Bruce Craig Historic Racing Photos)

The auto thrill show has been a longtime staple of summertime Americana at fairgrounds everywhere. A 1935 Ford plunges into a group of "catch" cars including a pair of Chevrolets and a Ford during a ramp launch exhibition. (Bruce Craig Historic Racing Photos)

Fans were seemingly everywhere watching Duke Nalon crash in the Aug. 24, 1941, 100-mile Championship Car race at the Wisconsin State Fair Park in West Allis. His Ziffrin Special hit the boards on the infield on lap 55. Nalon walked among the timber unhurt. (Phil Hall Collection)

A trip into the surrounding vegetation took June Cleveland out of a late-1940s stock car race at Lakewood Park in Atlanta, Ga. Cleveland was unhurt. Motoring past was Gober Sosebee (#50). (Phil Hall Collection)

Two unidentified drivers occupy the same part of the paved Soldier Field (Chicago) racing surface in this 1948 crash. The fans loved it, the drivers seemed less enthusiastic. (Phil Hall Collection)

Track roadsters, jalopies or whatever they were called were popular post-World War II attractions. This June 9, 1948, show at Soldier Field in Chicago played to a packed house. Gene Marmor (#6) finds himself involved in a three-car crash. Despite minimal safety equipment, there were no injuries. Note the speed equipment on the flathead engines. (Phil Hall Collection)

In the days before roll bars and roll cages, the roof of this 1949 Plymouth business coupe held up well enough to prevent driver Charles Parsieau from suffering serious injury when he flipped while qualifying for the July 10, 1949, stock car race at the Wisconsin State Fair Park in West Allis. (Phil Hall Collection)

Tony Bettenhausen got a bit too far inside and blasted a hay bale in an indoor midget race Jan. 20, 1951, at the Chicago International Amphitheater. He was trying to pass Myron Fohr, who went on to finish second. Undaunted, Bettenhausen captured third place. (Phil Hall Collection)

A pair of mid-1940s Chevrolet sedans were deemed fodder for a 1957 demolition derby at the Waukegan (Ill.) Speedway. The car in the foreground, which has seen contact, is about to alter the shape of the straight example behind. (Phil Hall Collection)

The driveable postwar Chrysler population around the Waukegan Speedway is in the process of being reduced by two as the result of this 1957 demolition derby at the track. The 10-or-so-year-old vehicles were seen as having little value at the time. (Phil Hall Collection)

Jalopy races were popular in the late 1940s and early 1950s. Composed mostly of prewar cars, the junkyard escapees crashed a lot. This three car pileup of Fords at the Frankville (Wis.) Speedway needed untangling. John Lundquist is shown climbing out of the top car. (Phil Hall Collection)

Thoughts of future collectibility were absent in 1959 when this pileup took place in a spectator race at the Cedarburg (Wis.) Raceway. Fritz Blazel got his 1951 Ford Victoria atop the rolling 1953 Dodge of Dale Koehler. Neither was injured. (Phil Hall Collection)

An urgent need to exit his 1955 Chevrolet (#51) was felt by Jim Cossman Sept. 1, 1962, at the Waukegan (Ill.) Speedway. This fiery crash occurred in the sportsman feature after Cossman's car was rear-ended by the 1955 Studebaker of Jim Getty (#A69), who also got out safely and quickly. (Phil Hall Collection)

The battered Novi Special driven by Paul Russo sat parked in the infield after his crash while leading the 1956 Indianapolis 500. He was not seriously hurt. (Phil Hall Collection)

Marshall Teague, better known for his stock car racing, crashed his AAA Championship car into the creek in the infield at the Wisconsin State Fair Park mile in West Allis on June 6, 1954. Teague was not seriously hurt. The same could not be said for the Fullerton Special, which had to be extracted from the shallow stream. Note the gentleman to the far left wearing the cowboy hat, famous car owner J.C. Agajanian of California. (Phil Hall Collection)

Three makes of stock cars got their exteriors torn up in this Aug. 23, 1959, crash in a 150-mile USAC event at Wisconsin State Fair Park in West Allis. Iggy Katona (#30) spun his 1958 Ford and collected Red Swanburg's 1957 Chevrolet (#10) and Bill Shoulder's 1958 Oldsmobile. Only the cars and pride were injured. (Phil Hall Collection)

A multi-car wreck in the July 12, 1964, 200-miler for USAC stock cars at the Wisconsin State Fair Park in West Allis eliminated front runner Lloyd Ruby (#18) in Norm Nelson's 1964 Plymouth. Ruby climbed from his battered mount and waited for the tow truck. Note the fuel leaking from the smashed tank. (Phil Hall Collection)

A.J. Foyt's ride in the Aug. 16, 1962, 200-mile USAC stock car race at the Wisconsin State Fair Park Speedway ended when he was involved in a crash that mangled his Ray Nichels' 1962 Pontiac. Foyt got out unharmed and (below) a wrecker crew looks for a place to hook up the bent car. (Phil Hall Collection)

Tom Cox severely shortened his 1961 Ford in the July 15, 1962, USAC 200-mile stock car race at the Wisconsin State Fair Park Speedway mile. Cox's Ford slammed the wall (top) in the north turn and nearly left the track. He was not hurt. The safety crew (center) rolls the tipped car back on its wheels before the wrecker crew (bottom) hooks it up to bring the crumpled Ford back to the pit area. (Phil Hall Collection)

Eddie Meyer (#55) hit the outside guard rail and flipped in the Sept. 6, 1964, USAC stock car race held at DuQuoin, Ill. Also involved in the incident with Meyer's 1964 Ford was Rodger Ward's 1964 Mercury. Ward is running off the track. Both drivers were uninjured. (Phil Hall Collection)

Art Tattersall exits his battered Volvo P-1800 after rolling it in the March 21, 1964, 12-hour event at Sebring, Fla. Tattersall was not seriously injured. Note the fuel leaking onto the trunk lid. (Phil Hall Collection)

Mak Kronn's Chevrolet-powered McKee leaves the track at Road America (Elkhart Lake, Wis.) via a Ford tow truck after a crash in the Sept. 4, 1966, Road America 500 sidelined him. The June Sprints winner tangled with Richard Dagiel's Lotus and spun, hitting Ralph Salyer's McKee, which ended up in the ditch. All drivers were okay. (Phil Hall Collection)

AUTOMOBILE SAFETY WAS NEVER "AD"-LIBBED

SAFETY PRODUCT PROMOTION THROUGH THE YEARS

AUTOMOBILE TRADE JOURNAL   157

Sell Them
4-Way Protection

That's what McKay Dealers are doing. In the McKay line they've got a lot of new bumper ideas to sell—many features that other bumpers lack.

Because of these McKay innovations they can offer the motorist full protection all around the car—front bumpers, side guards and rear bumpers.

Motorists are looking for "up-to-dateness" in the bumpers they buy—not "old stuff." And that's perfectly natural. You want the latest designs in everything you buy. So handle the new things in motor accessories and you'll be sure to sell them quickly and with profit to yourself.

The complete line of McKay Bumpers has many real advantages. Write for our bumper proposition.

UNITED STATES CHAIN & FORGING COMPANY
UNION TRUST BLDG., PITTSBURGH, PA.
*Makers of McKay Tire Chains, Shurout Chains, Ready Repair Links,
Bumpers and Chains for all industrial and commercial purposes.*

The McKay
Perfection Bumper
a new design
(reversed for rear)

McKAY RED BEAD BUMPERS
McK

1925 - McKay bumpers

IMPERIAL TELTAILITE

Teltailite sells rapidly because it is a necessity on any car. The type shown fits all models of Boyce Motometer except the Midget. Illustration shows view from the front. From the driver's seat, the Teltailite signal is seen directly behind the thermometer. Lights up when stoplight flashes and tells the driver that his stoplight is working properly.

No. 24-L Teltailite retails for $3.00

THE IMPERIAL BRASS MFG. CO.
1234 W. Harrison St.   Chicago

1925 - Imperial taillight

MORE THAN JUST CHAINS!
REAL ANTI-SKIDS!

Chains weren't made to prevent skidding. They were made to lift weights, tow cars, moor boats. Protex won't do any of these things satisfactorily, but they WILL prevent skidding. They were designed for the sole purpose of skid prevention and nothing else.

The horseshoe-edge links afford more friction surface and guard against skid IN ANY DIRECTION.

On the inside, Protex Chains present a broad, smooth surface that positively CANNOT injure the rubber. A real scientific anti-skid device. Get ready now for the new era of anti-skid protection. If your jobber can't supply you, write us direct, mentioning his name.

PROTEX CHAIN CO.
Waynesboro, Pa.

PROTEX TIRE CHAINS

1926 - Protex tire chains

The ADAMS Adjustable

Senior $3.50
Junior $1.25

FOOT-REST

Comes exactly in the natural position for every driver's foot. Adjustable to so many heights and angles that it fits any adult leg length. Selling now, time after time, from dealers' counters, on sight.

*Ask your jobber, or write us
direct, giving his name*

ADAMS MFG. COMPANY
Galesburg   Illinois

1925 - Adams foot rest

1915 - Seng horn switch

1926 - Saf-De-Light headlights

1926 - Wirebestos brake linings

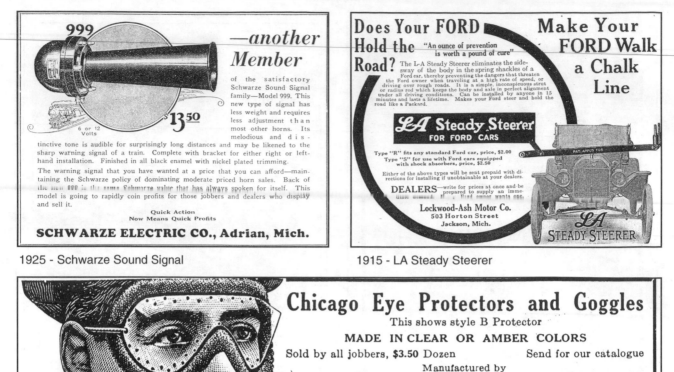
1925 - Schwarze Sound Signal

1915 - LA Steady Steerer

1913 - Chicago Eye Shield goggles

1926 - Bendix brakes

1926 - Johns-Manville brake linings

1926 - McKay tire chains

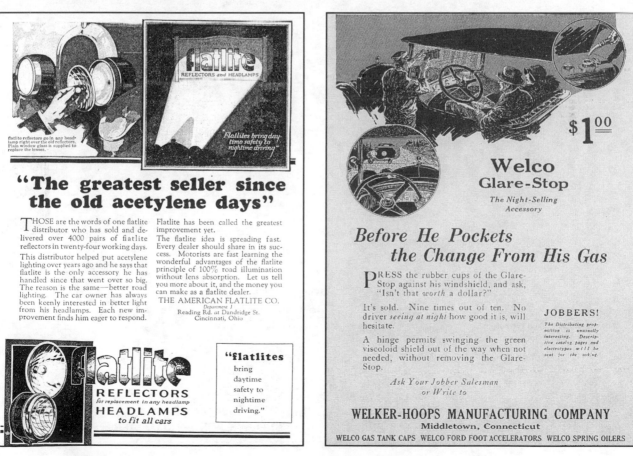

1925 - American Flatlite headlamp reflectors

1925 - Welco Glare-Stop shield

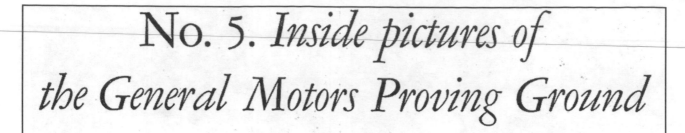

No. 5. *Inside pictures of the General Motors Proving Ground*

AT General Motors' 1268-acre Proving Ground in Michigan, automobiles are subjected to tests so rigid that the customary precision instruments were found inadequate. So the engineers have developed special devices and test methods which eliminate variables and measure the details of construction and performance with exactitude. The facts determined and studied with an Open Mind are used for the continuous improvement of General Motors cars.

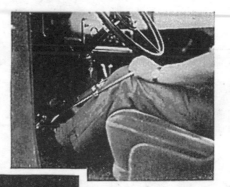

Above. The fuel consumption of a car is important to its owner. The Proving Ground device shown here measures this phase of performance—and so precisely that "miles per gallon" becomes virtually "drops per foot."

Below. This device is a telemeter, which measures vibration electrically and accurately. Another specially developed instrument, based on the principle of the microphone, measures noises within the car.

Above. This special instrument, developed by the Proving Ground engineers, measures clutch pedal pressure. Still other devices have been developed to record acceleration and deceleration to a degree of accuracy previously unknown.

Below. Steering ease is another big factor in safety and driving comfort. Shown here is a "duplicate" steering wheel which the engineers have developed to measure steering effort.

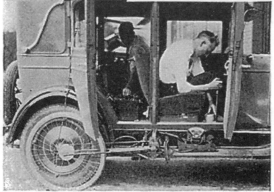

Above. The large picture shows a group of Proving Ground engineers examining the precision device described at the upper right. The "fifth wheel," shown at the rear wheel of the car, is another specially developed instrument which measures exact speed.

Altogether more than 135 different tests are employed at the Proving Ground in the separation of fact from opinion and the *proving* of General Motors cars.

"A car for every purse and purpose"

CHEVROLET · PONTIAC · OLDSMOBILE · MARQUETTE · OAKLAND · VIKING
BUICK · LA SALLE · CADILLAC · *All with Body by Fisher*
GENERAL MOTORS TRUCKS · YELLOW CABS *and* COACHES

1929 - General Motors Proving Ground testing

1937 - Goodrich Silvertown tires

"SAFETY INTERIORS" SENSATIONAL NEW IDEA IN MOTOR CAR SAFETY!

SMOOTH...all instrument board controls are recessed...lower edge of panel is rounded... soft rubber windshield-wiper knobs.

Every Detail Inside the Car Recessed or Padded or Redesigned for Protection of Passengers

HERE'S ONE of the most interesting improvements in 1937 automobiles...the handsome, new interiors of Plymouth cars...designed and planned for safety, as well as beauty.

This has been done, as a result of clinical research, to eliminate minor mishaps inside the car... bruises in case of sudden stops... torn clothing...barked knuckles.

SUDDEN STOP: No harm! The deep padding of the front seat is carried over the back edge in a heavy roll that prevents bumps.

The beautiful 1937 Plymouth De Luxe Four-Door Sedan

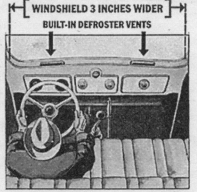

WINDSHIELD 3 INCHES WIDER
BUILT-IN DEFROSTER VENTS

BETTER VISION AHEAD...the ventilating windshield is clear, and wider by 3". Warm air defroster vents built in.

SAFER—AND EASIER! Driving the new Plymouth is effortless. Easiest steering you have ever experienced; easy, quiet gear shifting; no sway on curves. Plus big, double-action hydraulic brakes that stop you smoothly, *safely!*

WHAT MAKES A SAFE CAR

★ DOUBLE-ACTION HYDRAULIC BRAKES...self-equalizing ...sure, swift, safe stops.

★ ALL-STEEL BODY...the top is one solid "stamping" of steel...walls, doors, floor are *all steel* reinforced with steel.

★ EFFORTLESS STEERING... responds to a touch...no sway on curves. Driving is really restful; parking's a cinch!

★ NO SWAY ON CURVES...rigid stabilizer at front end of extra-rigid frame keeps car on even keel...steady on the turns.

★ SAFETY INTERIOR...every detail carefully styled and designed for greater safety as well as beauty.

LOW FLOORS—No "hump" in rear. Wide doors. "Chair-height" seats that support your whole body properly...and permit you to ride in restful, relaxed comfort.

HEAR A WATCH TICK! Big all-steel body is sound-proofed like a modern broadcasting studio. Noise shut out...prevents nerve-strain and fatigue...another big safety factor.

EASY TO BUY

You'll discover this beautiful, new 1937 Plymouth is priced with the lowest...and offers a payment plan which will fit your budget. See your Chrysler, De Soto or Dodge dealer—for the convenient purchase terms made available by the Commercial Credit Company...terms as low as $25 a month. PLYMOUTH DIVISION OF CHRYSLER CORPORATION, Detroit, Mich.

1937 - Plymouth safety interiors

Torture-Tests Show Why Today's Cars are Safer

FEW PEOPLE KNOW about these almost unbelievable tests. Yet they make Plymouth *"the car that stands up best."* And it's priced with the lowest...with Commercial Credit Company's easy terms offered by Dodge, DeSoto and Chrysler dealers.

1 **Punishment in a Sandpit.** This Plymouth is taking a cruel beating on wheels, transmission, steering mechanism...much worse than any owner will ever give it.

2 **Tortured on a "Twist Rack."** Powerful jacks give the frame terrific inequalities of pressure at four corners. Yet the body stays level...proving the strength of Plymouth's big X-braced frame.

3 **2000 lbs. Tension** tries to separate the steel-and-rubber bond of a Floating Power engine mounting.

4 **Ten Solid Days of "Bumps"** is what this spring has taken—and it's still going strong! Plymouth's springs are Amola steel...they stand up better.

5 **No—He Won't Fall Through.** The safety glass of the windshield is supporting the man's entire weight. When he drops that steel ball, the glass will crack...but it *won't* crash!

6 **Sandbagging** a steering wheel. It delivers a blow of 3000 inch-pounds. Plymouth's steering wheels must resist this abuse.

7 **The "Belgian Roll"** is the most vicious of all tests. It shakes and joggles the whole car. It deals out strains, bumps, twists, vibration. Stock Plymouths must meet these tests.

8 **10° Below Zero**—Plymouth engines start quickly and easily...in every extreme of weather.

9 **The Big 1938 Plymouth** has long life built into every part. See it today. PLYMOUTH DIVISION OF CHRYSLER CORPORATION, Detroit, Mich. Major Bowes' Amateur Hr., C.B.S. Network, Thurs., 9-10 p.m., E.S.T

COMPARE VALUES OF "ALL THREE" **Plymouth Builds Great Cars**

1938 - Plymouth torture testing

1953 - Saginaw power steering

THE WORLD'S LARGEST SELLING V·8
...and Lifeguard Design is another reason why!

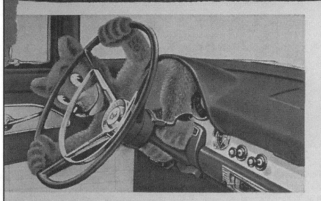

This Lifeguard steering wheel has a new deep-center construction to reduce possibility of driver being thrown hard against steering post in case of accident. Ford engineers have mounted the rim of the wheel high above the recessed steering post to help "cushion" your chest against severe injuries from impact.

Optional Lifeguard padding protects you against accident injuries by providing a "crash cushion" on both the instrument panel and sun visors. It is five times more shock absorbent than foam rubber. New Lifeguard rearview mirror that "gives" on impact and resists shattering is standard on '56 models.

You're twice as safe if you stay inside the car in an accident. Statistics prove it conclusively. So our Ford engineers have designed these new Lifeguard door latches with a *double grip* to reduce the possibility of doors springing open in a collision.

Look at this Ford seat belt! One-third stronger than required for airlines, it is securely anchored to reinforced, all-steel floor structure. Optional Ford seat belts can be adjusted or released with one hand . . . are available in colors to harmonize with interiors.

THE NEW FORDOR VICTORIA

"And you'll drive safer ever after!"

FORD V·8
Sells More because it's Worth More!

1956 - Ford Lifeguard Design features

Paul Schneider of Hillsdale, Mich., writes: "One of my co-workers had parked his Chevrolet at home, got out, walked away, and then watched as it backed down the hill and hit a guy wire dead center to do a balancing act. This happened back in the mid-1960s." (Paul Schneider photo)

Evidence, facts, experience, inescapable conclusions have been accumulating on highway safety. The new view, unlike the old shoulder-shrugging, nothing-can-be-done-about-it attitude, declares that something can be done about highway safety -- that something must be done. And something is being done. The new view says we can have the automobile and free travel on this nation's far-reaching highways; and with that privilege, safety.

Seven Roads to Safety - 1939

Paul G. Hoffman (president of Studebaker)

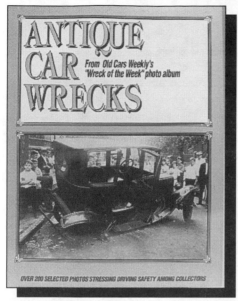
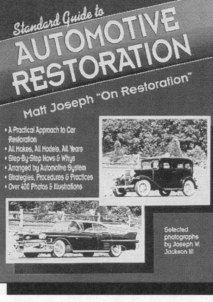
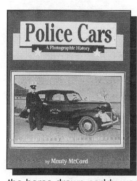
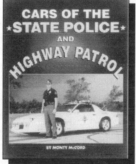

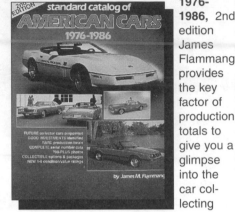

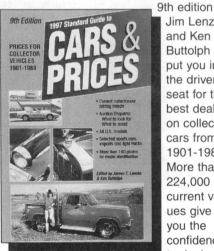
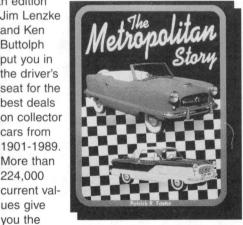
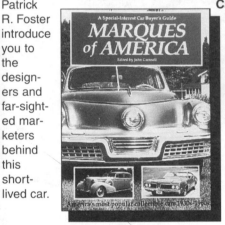